£2.00.

GW00455147

SHANNOCKS IN WARTIME

The Town Clock in War Weapons Week, 1942

Shannocks
in
Wartime

May Ayers

author of
Memoirs of a Shannock

*This book is dedicated to the memory of
my brother Bob and my sister Ena.*

Larks Press

Published by the
Larks Press
Ordnance Farmhouse
Guist Bottom, Dereham, Norfolk NR20 5PF
01328 829207

March 2001

Printed by the Lanceni Press
Garrood Drive, Fakenham

British Library Cataloguing-in-Publication Data
A catalogue record for this book is available
from the British Library.

Photographs taken by H.H.Tansley during the war
were inherited by Mr Peregrine Long
who has generously given them to the
Sheringham Museum.

ISBN 0 948400 96 X

Foreword

Authors of local history books fall into two basic categories: those who have some knowledge of an area and strengthen this with detailed research into the community's history, customs, development and personalities, and those who write from a deep personal knowledge based on growing up through childhood, formative teen years and adulthood in their home town or village. May Ayers, a true 'shannock', belongs in the latter category.

In this book she gives us a highly personalised account of her memories and experiences during the war 1939 to 1945. She brings to life what it was like to court and marry a man from foreign parts – Lowestoft –the anxiety whilst he was away on active service, the terror of surviving air-raids and a general flavour of what life was like in Sheringham during those dark days.

It is a story which complements her earlier book, *Memoirs of a Shannock,* and should find a place on the bookshelf of everyone interested in the story of Sheringham and its people.

Peter Brooks

Introduction

The days of our youth come back so vividly as we grow older that perhaps we view them through rose-tinted glasses. We recall especially the happy years and the friends that we knew then.

In 1939, we were young and carefree, on the threshold of life; pleasures were simple and money scarce. With the onset of the war all that was to change. Some who had never before left the town were transported to far-away lands, some never to return. On that day, September 3rd, our world was turned upside down. We did not know what would happen, but always a certain spirit seemed to carry us through the dreary days. It is difficult to describe the comradeship that prevailed throughout those years, helped us through the joys and sadness of each passing day and enabled us to do our best in all circumstances.

In this little book I have not been able to do full justice to the spirit and atmosphere that was everywhere at the time. The things that happened to me, happened to so many others all over the country: young people married only to part and meet again when fate decided, and those fortunate enough to survive look back on it all with pride.

Acknowledgements

My grateful thanks must go to the following people who kindly gave their time and were willing to provide me with various dates and names:

to my son, Christopher Ayers, who transferred my hand-written chapters on to computer disk, for his valuable time and helpful suggestions:

to David Craske of Sheringham for his help and the use of his photographs of the bombing of Cromer Road, New Road, Beeston Road and Priory Road, and the Town Clock war bonds, and for information about the evacuation of the school children to various houses in the town, which was confirmed by Geoffrey Paice:

to Charles Postle for his help with the names of assistants at C.T.Bakers of Sheringham, to Ronnie Wright for information about the early days of C. A. Sadlers and Blyth and Wrights, Ironmongers and

to Peter Brooks, who was kind enough to read my first draft and who has provided the Foreword.

6

1. How things were

It is hard to visualize the changes that have taken place over the last seventy years in the little town of Sheringham where I was born. Today the summer months bring crowds of holiday-makers who come to enjoy the North Norfolk Coast. The small streets are full of traffic and the tourists bring business to the shops and a sense of prosperity.

My generation enjoyed a slower pace of life, when the streets and alleyways echoed to the sound of children playing simple games. Ours were the days of the horse and cart, soon followed by the older members out with their buckets or barrows, gathering up any droppings for their back gardens or allotments.

The town was very small and nearly everyone knew everyone else. Here and there would be groups of landladies exchanging a word or two. Usually they wore aprons over long black skirts and shawls around their shoulders for comfort; with their black hats and little black boots they were the essence of respectability.

There was a large linen shop (now Stead & Simpsons) run by Miss Cross and her two assistants with a ground floor and a spacious first floor. Here you could buy a splendid array of linens, crash and woven materials; large cabinets held embroidery wools, silks, chintz, flowered materials and paper transfers.

Next door to this was C. T. Baker's the ironmongers and, on the other side of the linen shop, was a large store called Pages of Aylsham, a delightful shop in my younger days. At Christmas time they always had windows full of toys and presents, and we children would stare through the windows hoping for something like them in our Christmas stockings. It was a brightly-lit shop and at Christmas a large tree, decorated with candles and toys stood just inside the main door.

These shops would remain open on Saturday nights and one Christmas, running across the road from Starlings opposite in the dark to see Pages' window, I was almost knocked down by the 'midnight milkman's' horse and cart. My brother Bob hauled me to safety saying, 'What ever are you thinking about? You could have been knocked down, then you wouldn't have had any Christmas!'.

One Christmas, my sister, Ena, took me along to see all the dolls. She kept asking me which one I liked; there were so many on display with long hair and golden curls, but the one I wanted was an ordinary doll with short bobbed hair and a sweet smile. My sister tried hard to persuade me to look at all the other dolls, but I only had eyes for the one that seemed a bit lonely. So there in my stocking on Christmas morning was the one I had longed for.

Pages had a ground floor and a staircase to the first floor, where all manner of goods could be bought, ladies outfits and millinery, lino, carpets, rugs, bed-linen, haberdashery, cotton materials, and woollen goods. Another department was for high-class provisions, with chairs to sit on, a desk with a lady cashier, and errand boys to deliver goods to their valued customers.

Later on, an arcade was built, which was a great advantage as customers could view the various items under cover. Later in my life, when a Miss Plews was manageress, I was employed there; today this is Craske's Restaurant, and the building has not been much altered.

Across the road was Starlings Emporium, not so large as it is today, but a very popular place for its toys and games, newspapers and miscellaneous goods. In our younger days there was a large wooden building at the rear where we often went to a magic lantern show or a concert.

Rounce and Wortleys, another newspaper shop, which also stocked photographs and greetings cards, was in Church Street not many doors from Bertram Watts, who sold toys, books, games and stationery. He also had a lending library upstairs, very popular with visitors, for one could borrow a book for a few pennies. Part of Bertram Watts present shop was the old post office, a fairly large office to the right of the present shop; a staircase divided the two premises which I believe led up to some offices above.

Another large store, on the corner opposite the Town Clock, was Jarrolds of Norwich, selling china and glass ornaments as well as newspapers, stationery, and cards. They also had a lending library. This area of the store was narrow, all the books on shelves behind the outside window facing into Station Road; the entrance to the shop was up two steps at the corner of the building. (This is now the Little Theatre and coffee bar.)

Another fine shop was Hughes & Bailey's in Church Street, which sold clocks, watches and jewellery. All the shops had chairs

8

for the customers to sit on. Everything was done at a more genteel and leisurely pace in those days and the customer was very much considered and appreciated. Dora Brookes' shop in Church Street was very fashionable, catering for ladies of ample means who led a more leisurely life.

Gilbert's shop in High Street was another small store that sold special brands of provisions. Inside the door, was the customary desk with its lady attendant who dealt with all payments. Mr Gilbert was the Chairman of the Town Council and was well respected; his shop employed four or five staff, and he was always willing to deliver goods and provided an errand boy for this and later on a van.

C.A. Sadler's, the predecessor of Blyth & Wright's
In 1933 Messrs Blyth and Wright took over Sadler's business. They delivered paraffin and kindling and mended saucepans and kettles. This has been a family firm for three generations.

Blyth & Wright's store has always occupied the same site, but it was not as large before the war as it is today. Sheringham had a good supply of butchers' shops, Youngs, Arthurs, Dennis's etc, as well as suppliers of good-quality fresh fish.

Everywhere were seen the rugged fishermen in their colourful garb, thumping up and down the stones on the beach or the gang-

9

Sheringham High Street before the war

way, wearing their yellow oilskins and long thigh-boots. Most wore sou'westers and some fishermen preferred to wear them back to front. Carrying their peds (baskets) of cod, crabs & lobsters, they would be surrounded by eager visitors who delighted to watch their activities. They were reluctant to converse when busy, and some fishermen could be inclined to be surly, but in the occasional idle moment they could be quite the opposite, enthralling all and sundry with exciting tales.

Some of the older fishermen, now long gone, Bennett Middleton, Jimmy Dumble and especially 'Chicken' Grice, could pull the wool over your eyes with incredible tales. It was always a problem to tell whether they were pulling a fast one or if it was real. Many a one was hoaxed by their yarns and sense of humour.

There were many large boats in those days, hovellers and whelkers. The West End beaches and gangway would hold 20 to 30 boats; some were also at the Admiralty slope but this was a very vulnerable place. Along at the East beach there would be 10 or more large boats. There was much activity when boats were being winched across the sand, hand-made barrows at the ready. They were filled with the latest catch and wheeled off to the particular merchant they dealt with, 'Old Chibbles' Bishop' perhaps, or

10

Henry 'Downtide' West or Old John Long. The fishermen went to sea, two or three in a boat, partners together, and often kept with the same fish-merchant for years. Then some tried to be more business-like and sent their catches off by railway to London

No longer do we see the robust groups of fishermen here and there about the town. Gone are the old familiar faces we knew, most of them with snow-white beards. They would gather in large groups 'eyeing the weather' strutting up and down and flapping their arms across their chests. They would argue, gesticulate, and remonstrate with one another over conditions of the weather, football, religion and local topics with now and again angry words. On a Sunday evening, there they would be, sheltered in the lea of a shop, waiting for the Salvation Army band to appear for its evening open-air service. There would be some near the Town Clock, and another lot in the doorway of the International Stores at the bottom of the High Street where they would watch the band as it marched back to barracks.

Photo: Clive Hedges

Sheringham Town Clock before the war

These men were always dressed in their navy hand-knitted 'ganseys', (Guernseys) dark grey or black trousers (wide-bottomed), wearing their best 'go-to-meeting' clothes on the sabbath, and 'slops'. Today we hardly see a single descendant of those men wearing a fisherman's gansey; times have changed. In my youth it was extremely difficult to get my father or brother to

11

wear a shirt and necktie; always they insisted on wearing the traditional gear, smart and well-dressed on a Sunday or to a funeral, but never a necktie, only what they called a 'wrapper' (pronounced wropper), a silk scarf worn around the neck. When my dear old father had to wear a shirt and necktie in a residential home, he was most put out, saying, 'Wuz this thing I've got on?' pointing to his shirt and tie. He was a bit happier when I said how smart he looked, but he still protested, 'Never see such ole stuff where ever hev it come from?'

One remaining character in the town today, who still wears the traditional gear is Lenny 'Teapot' West, and he does try to stick to the old traditions.

A favourite place for the fishermen to congregate was on West Cliff, in the lea of Tom Perry's sweet shop and ice-cream store. They would line up here and study the weather, taking a look at the 'weather glass' and the state of the tide. In those early years Tom's mother had this place, handy for the visitors on the nearby prom, but also an ideal lea against the wind in whatever direction.

When the bridge over the gangway was built, it made another vantage point where twenty or more older ones, their days now finished at sea, would be watching for the boats to come home. One could be sure of a gathering here at any time of the year, especially when the weather was rough, but times have changed. It is hard to find a group of fishermen these days and those who still try to make a living at sea must feel a certain sadness.

On the east side of the town it was much the same; on the promenade, were two or more sitting places, where both young and old fishermen would be seen braiding pots, mending nets, or just gazing out to sea. Here on the stones would be as many as seven or eight large boats, and other smaller ones. This would be a hive of activity, boats coming ashore and being winched across the sand to unload their catches, a great area for the visitors to the town, as at any time of the day you could see fishermen involved in their everyday tasks. Boats could also be hired to take off fishing parties or pleasure-trippers. Youths were employed to walk or cycle along the beaches selling ice-cream, chocolates, sweets and drinks. In those days most of the wooden breakwaters had large wooden steps for easy access, so you could walk quite easily along the beaches in any direction without leaving the sand, especially when the tide was out.

2. Yesterday's Memories

About 1921 or 1922 we were living in Cremer Street and just two doors away, at Vine Cottage, were Levi Cox and his wife, who were distantly related to my mother. They had three sons, Willie, Martin and Frank; they also had two young nieces who lived in Norwich and whenever they came to Sheringham they would come in to see us. I remember I was playing with some toys when one of their family came running in saying,

'You must come and hear our wireless.' Whereupon I was quickly gathered up and carried in to Levi's and promptly placed on a high chair at their dining room table. There in front of me was a small box-like article and one of the boys was twiddling with a bit of wire (I think these were called the 'cat's whiskers'). While he was connecting this up to a cylinder, they hurriedly put some large earphones on my head and said excitedly, 'Can't you hear anything?' I could just hear, from a great distance, a kind of tapping, no music at all. Again they said, 'Can't you hear them? They're clapping in the Albert Hall.' I was a bit mystified as Albert Hall meant nothing to me, but this was my first taste of radio.

It was many years before we had our first wireless. All my close friends, then fifteen to sixteen years old, were singing the latest songs and talking about the band-leaders, but I was quite in the dark. I didn't like to show my ignorance, so I was glad when my father decided we would have a radio, naturally to help them with the weather forecasts. Most of the fisherman by this time had acquired wireless sets to help them when they went to sea.

We had a Pilot radio at first because this had a Marine Band and we could listen to the shipping forecast and regularly tune into the various lightships that were stationed all along the North Norfolk Coast, from the Lynn Well to Yarmouth. We became quite familiar with the voices of the men on the Cross sands, Haisbro, Inner and Outer Dowsing, giving out the state of the weather as they talked to the coastguards. We could hear the trawlers calling each other up and remarking about their catches. If they got too blasphemous, my father would switch off. We could also hear these vessels talking by radio link to those at home. To operate a radio in those far off days we depended on batteries connected to the set, and they had to be recharged every so often; they were quite heavy to carry and had to be taken to one of the people who did this in the town, Hunt's shop opposite the top of New Road or Major Dunn's further along toward the High Street. The charge only lasted about a week or ten days but we kept taking them to be re-charged for many years.

Photo: Popperfoto

**Henry 'Downtide' West serving Mabel Dumble
at the wet fish shop
(Major Dunn's in the background)**

Cars were not seen in the streets in my early days. Horses and carts still predominated, delivering all manner of goods about the town. Cars were slowly coming in, and those who had profitable businesses were just beginning to get vans or lorries and taxis for the holiday-makers.

14

There were barrow boys about the streets, and High Street traders like Sid Hastings and 'Fruit' Cooper had the initiative to augment their shop income by supplying people with goods from a hand-cart or barrow; this brought in extra income and also allowed the landladies and the proprietors of the hotels easier access.

Most of the visitors to the town in those days arrived by train; very few owned cars. Their luggage arrived the day before and was delivered to the houses where they were to stay by horse-drawn carts belonging to the railway. The *Norfolkman* and the *Broadsman*, passenger trains that travelled from London to Sheringham in about three hours, ran every day throughout the summer months.

My first car ride was when I was eight years old. A family from Leicester came to our house to stay each year - I believe their name was Shepheard. This particular year, 1925, they came by car, and one day the gentleman asked my father whether he would like a little ride and 'perhaps your little daughter would like to come too?' I was pleased to be included in the outing. Outside our house stood the little car, a small red one. My father was invited to sit alongside the driver. I was puzzled as to where I was going to sit, as I couldn't see another seat anywhere for me. Suddenly, the gentleman went to the back of the car and pulled up a part of the rear to reveal a 'dickey' seat. Father lifted me in, and out in the fresh air I felt quite safe as we didn't go very fast - it was most enjoyable.

My first ride on a motor-bike, however, was far from enjoyable. My sister, who was in service in London, regularly came home for her holidays to stay with us, and when she brought home the young man she was engaged to, they arrived on a very powerful motor-bike. The next day he said he would give me a ride to Blakeney and back. We went to Blakeney all right, but on the return journey I was holding on to him for dear life, the water streaming from my eyes, no goggles, not even a scarf. As we arrived back home he casually said, 'Well that wasn't bad, we were doing over 60 miles an hour!' I made no comment, but just managed to stagger indoors on wobbly legs.

There were times when horses could be just as frightening as motor-bikes. I am reminded of the summer when a little girl called Joy Pullinger and her mother came to stay next door for the whole of the holidays. She was a very pretty little girl and much enjoyed coming into our house. Whenever I went to the shops at the bottom of our road she loved to come with me. I was going to go

15

to the Co-operative Stores at the end of the road and Joy wanted to come with me, so I took her hand and away we went.

Suddenly, I heard a rattling and rumbling noise coming from the far end of Cremer Street, and as I looked in the direction of the noise I noticed a horse and cart coming out from the old council yard. I then realized that the horse was bolting and there was no one in charge of it. The street was empty and I was just alongside Johnny Johnson's (now the old boathouse) with the little girl. I didn't know what to do or where to go. I was still quite young, but I knew if I tried to return to the safety of our house I might not make it. What could I do? The horse and cart were nearly upon me, travelling very fast. I pulled Joy as close as I could to the wooden railings, putting myself on the other side of her. By this time the horse and cart were upon us; all I could see were the legs and flanks of the horse as it thundered along the guttering of the pavement. If it hadn't been for the pavement the runaway cart would have hit us. I'm sure the high kerb saved us. The poor frightened animal tried to turn at the bottom of the road, but it collided with the wooden fencing and a workshop and booking office belonging to Mr Wordingham in Co-operative Street, pulling them down with it. It was a lucky escape for us and quite alarming, but the little girl wasn't frightened at all as she hardly realized what was happening.

There where quite a few runaway horses and carts in those days – and runaway animals. Living quite near the slaughter-house in Hastings Lane, we would often see the men trying to recapture pigs or bullocks that had managed to get away in a dash for freedom.

My father loved walking in the woods and often of a Sunday morning he would take me with him. I loved these walks because he seemed to know every tree and bush and could name them; he certainly knew where the best chestnut or hazel-nut trees were, whether in the Springs Woods or in the larger expanse of woods that stretched east of the town above the hills of Beeston Regis as far as Roman Camp. He called these woods the 'Canadies', and said they were called this because a man called Canady had been buried deep in the heart of them. I always felt a bit scared whilst there as they were so large and dark and creepy.

In early September, when Mother had gone to Chapel, Father would say, 'Come on, let's go and get filberts.' These were hazel nuts, but later on it would be chestnuts. One of his local nicknames was 'Old Nuts' as he certainly loved them.

On our way along the main Cromer Road we had to pass Reynolds barn, just south of the Priory. Lying just outside this barn (now demolished) near the large barn doors were three or four very large granite stones, perhaps old marker stones, and as we got alongside them he would say to me, 'See those old stones? They go across the road when they hear the cock crow.' I found this very interesting and pondered on it quite seriously as we made our way towards Britons Lane. Now and then I would remark on it, climbing the hill towards the wood, but he wouldn't make any comment about the stones, just left me to think. In the large woods, gathering nuts I would forget all about it, but on the way back, as we got to the barn, he would ask me if I could work out how they got across the road. Of course I couldn't, and he would quietly say, 'Well of course they can't hear the cock crow can they?'

Farmer Reynolds lived at the farmhouse with his wife Mary, and when he was buried at Beeston Church one of the largest stones was used to mark his grave and has his name engraved on it.

Although my father was only a fisherman and descended from six or seven generations of fishermen, he had a great love of nature. He was no gardener, however, and took no interest in the small back garden we had. My mother valiantly tried to grow plants and flowers in the sandy soil, and once I remember the little bank to the chapel at the bottom of our garden had several primroses growing quite bravely, but he came ashore one day and placed some worn out crab-pots on them, much to the dismay of my mother.

'Willie, look what you've done to my primroses!'

'Well primroses won't get your bread and butter,' he said.

One winter's night about 1928, father had been to look at the sea, and he came in to say, 'Come on, put your warm clothes on and come along o' me to see the Northern Lights.' I had seen these mysterious and colourful lights at times when they were briefly showing, but I had never seen the full glory of the Aurora Borealis before that time, nor have I since; it was the most spectacular display to behold. January or February is the most likely time to see them, but modern neon lights blot out the display and the wonders of the night sky. In those days the streets were only lit by

17

gas-lamps, so many areas of the town were quite dark. Of course there were no lights on the promenade, just the red light on the sea wall, so my father and I headed for the promenade to walk under the large sea wall, well wrapped up against the biting wind.

At first all that could be seen was a brilliant light on the northern horizon. The sea before us was very dark but, looking out to the north, this brilliant light began to enlarge; colours of purple, orange, and green, dazzling and dancing, reached higher and higher in the night sky. As we walked to the westward they became like an ever-changing curtain of every colour imaginable, rippling, swaying, high above our heads.

The sky to the south was dark and the sea calm. As the radiance increased, the whole of the sky, from the horizon line to the far south, was enveloped in curtains of colour, ever moving and changing; only a small portion of the night sky was dark. We stood amazed at the sight, I am sure that my father had never seen a display like this, orange, scarlet, blue, yellow and green, a most spectacular sight. As we reached the end of the promenade the coloured bands were directly over our head, blotting out the night sky. The magnificence of the Northern Lights on that special night has ever remained in my memory.

We took the *Daily Mail* newspaper at that time and on the following day it was reported that these magnificent lights had been seen all over the country.

Chapter 3. Our Youthful Days

Our school days ended when we were fourteen years old, unless we were lucky enough to pass the scholarship exam at the age of eleven and go to the grammar school, Paston for boys or North Walsham High School for girls. Some of my friends did this and one in particular, Gertie Dunn, went finally to Girton College, Cambridge. She was always a brainy girl and became a teacher herself, but those of us who had just average intelligence remained at the Sheringham Elementary School.

These were the days of the great depression in 1931. When I left school in the summer of that year quite a number of my friends had passed a second scholarship exam and were off to North Walsham High School. I knew I was going to miss them and things would not be the same, but now I was in the adult world and had to find a job, which wasn't so easy. There were hundreds of people out of work; we heard stories of the Jarrow marches, not really appreciating the great problem people had to make a living during that summer. Naturally I helped my mother with her holiday visitors, but in those days we didn't demand money - we knew the difficulty our parents had in feeding and clothing us, so didn't expect a wage for any work we did. I think we all knew that if we worked hard there would be some kind of recompense.

My sister Ena was earning fairly good money and was in service in London, so when she came home at the end of the summer she would take me off to Norwich to buy me perhaps a blazer, a skirt and blouse. One year I remember going with my sister to Norwich with her current boy friend who needed to go to the cattle market; this time I was bought a very beautiful tweed winter coat, much appreciated by me. It was a delight to go to Norwich on a football excursion train for 2s. 6d. return fare, have our afternoon tea in Princes Restaurant and go to Woolworths, the 3d. and 6d. store. For me it was like going into Aladdin's cave; I generally received a sixpenny box of paints and a painting book.

Things were far worse for those people who had eight or nine children to feed. Boys would take jobs as caddy boys on the golf links, doing two or three rounds a day for a well-off golfer, who might be generous and give a good tip, but most often were just 'thrupenny and sixpenny' tippers.

Boys who belonged to a fishing family would automatically go to sea for a living; it was the recognized thing to do and they had no other choice. A few who wanted to go to sea, and expected to do so, were put to another trade or profession, like Bob Rushmer who served in Pages' shop for many years.

Girls as they left school either went into service, leaving home and family to be taken on as a kitchen maid or housemaid for a pittance in the cities, or took shop jobs for the summer, or were apprenticed, receiving a very low wage.

My first job was at Jordan's the chemist where I stayed for only one week before leaving to go to work at Brenner's Bazaar. This was most enjoyable as there were about ten of us employed here and we all knew one another. Our wages were about 15 shillings a week. I gave my mother 10 shillings of this and, after insurance stamps, I had four shillings and sixpence for everything else. I seemed to manage all right, as I could go the cinema or buy a pair of stockings for 9d. and buy a bar of chocolate for 2d. We didn't have our hair done at the hairdressers very often, and had very few luxuries, but out of our money we always managed somehow to buy family and friends small presents. We were all in the same boat so we never envied each other.

After working for Mr Brenner I went to work for Alec Jeary in his vegetable shop. Then my father broke his ankle whilst working on the promenade and I had to leave Mr Jeary's to help my mother at home looking after visitors.

When the summer was over, my friend Bronny, who worked at Mr George Roe's hairdressers' in Station Road, had a better job offered to her as cash assistant at the desk at George Young's butcher's shop. She said, 'Why don't you go and get my place at the hairdressers?' Luckily, they took me on; the wages were about the same but gradually increased. Mr and Mrs Roe were very nice, genteel people to work for and I stayed with them until the outbreak of war in 1939. It was a very high-class salon, dealing with both ladies and gentlemen. These were the days of Marcel waving, when perms were only just coming in. They both attended to their customers with pomards, manicuring, shampoos and sets, styling etc. I was told to greet the clientèle with 'Good morning Madam or Sir,' and to say 'Good afternoon, Sir. Thank you.' My duties were to take all appointments or cancellations over the phone, keep both cubicles immaculately clean, and prepare the perms. Working there at that time was a friend from Brenner's Bazaar days, Doris Hack; we got on very well together. Her job was to keep the upstairs living quarters clean and tidy, also the living room and kitchen area. She would make coffee for us at 11 o'clock.

I remember Mr and Mrs Roe for their genteel manners; they always addressed each other as 'Mr Roe' or 'Mrs Roe' never using their forenames. It was a pleasure to work for them, but at the outbreak of war they felt they could only keep one of us and decided they were going to try to manage without me and keep Doris. So I went to the Employment Exchange and had a job offered me at Woolworths in Cromer, just for the Christmas period; it was hard work for little pay, about threepence per hour - I was glad when Christmas was over.

Later on that year, Mr Roe sent for me to go back to work for them again as Doris could not manage to do all the work. I was very happy to do this and I stayed until a better job came along. as manageress to a shop in Cromer called Flotsam & Jetsam. This was an excellent job at wages of 30 shillings per week, working for the two Miss Allens. I went on the bus at 10 o'clock, didn't start work until 10.30 and at 3.30 in the afternoon could go home. It was a very attractive little shop in Jetty Street, and sometimes I had to deliver items to customers, so I was not in the shop all day, but somehow I felt homesick. It was quite ridiculous as I was only five miles from Sheringham, but it seemed as if I was miles away. I stayed with them a couple of years and then, when another job came up in Sheringham at less money, I took it.

We had no money for luxuries and there was little transport that we could afford. If we wanted to get anywhere we either walked or cycled. A great many of my friends were able to have the use of a bike and, on our free days, about a dozen of us would go out cycling. There was little traffic on the roads and we could go riding around visiting our relations who lived in the country. When I first met the young man I was to marry, he would come to ours to stay and we would cycle to Great Aunt Polly who lived at Wickmere. She had a country cottage and garden with a well outside the door. There was always home-made wine brewing, and their little garden provided them with practically everything.

21

We certainly didn't have a great social life, but we would walk to Holt sometimes to see the Holt boys or they would walk to see us. It was the same with the Kelling and Salthouse fraternity, the only way we could get anywhere was to cycle or walk.

My brother Bob and his friend Robin Farrow had two girls they were interested in who both lived somewhere near Aldborough Green, so they would often be busy getting their bikes ready for a jaunt out. It was exasperating for them when they couldn't get their carbide lamps to light; they needed a lot of attention and there would be plenty of swearing before they left.

One of the Holt boys, Bert Woodrow, was sometimes lucky enough to get over to Sheringham on the back of his brother's motor-bike, and we would meet them. It may seem strange, but we never went over to Cromer to see the Cromer boys. I remember one night some Cromer lads came over and we got talking to them. Mentioning this incident to my father the next day, he said, 'What! Cromer? What ever do you mean, talking to the Cromer boys?'

I went out with Bert for a time, a very nice chap, younger than me, but sadly he later joined the R.A.F. and was lost over Germany during the war.

I well remember seeing the German Zeppelin *Hindenberg*, which came over our garden in Cremer Street; the lettering on the side was in red and done in italics. I also saw the R101 airship when she came newly out of her hangar and passed over the town at Easter 1931. I was in the queue at the fish shop in Windham Street, and, hearing the roar of engines, we all rushed outside to see her overhead, floating like a silver cigar above us.

I was about fourteen years old when Alan Cobham came to Norfolk and flights were offered at five shillings a trip. As usual none of us had enough money to do this, but my friend Margaret calmly told us that she had got enough money for a flight. Well, we all accompanied Margaret to the field where this was taking place, at the top of Britons Lane, just at the junction with the main Cromer Road. She went ahead while we all waited in the lane adjoining the field. Suddenly the two-winged plane took off and we scattered as, flying very low, it just skimmed the trees and bushes. It made a very small flight and back again; Margaret came back to us nonchalantly as if it were a daily occurrence.

Margaret and her auntie lived very near to the East Beach, in a house that overlooked the fishermen's beach, where they were always attending to fish and crabs and cutting up their bait. Auntie got very angry with the fishermen because of the smells that wafted up to her windows and she wrote many irate letters to the Council complaining about this. For a time it would improve, then it would lapse again until another angry letter to the Sheringham Council got something done. Mr Joshua Henry West (my grandfather) was approached by the Clerk of the Council to intercede with the fishermen to do their utmost to prevent this happening again.

Margaret and her aunt enjoyed swimming a great deal and went daily to the East Beaches for their dip. One evening I was with them on the beach just in front of their house and Margaret was just getting out of the water when a youth threw a large stone, which struck her on the right forehead. It made a very large cut and there was blood everywhere. Pandemonium reigned for a little while, but the beach inspectors soon appeared. In those days, the inspectors were extremely strict, and the youth was cautioned and his parents told. It all ended reasonably well, but Margaret always had the scar to show for the episode - in the shape of a fish!

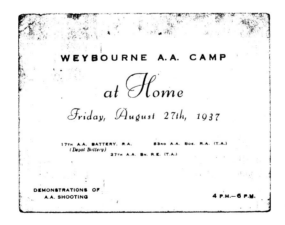

About 1936 Weybourne Camp, first established as a training camp for the territorials in the 1920s, became a special training ground for ack ack gunners. Young men from all areas arrived for two weeks of training. There were military personnel stationed there permanently to put all these young men through their paces; many were auxiliaries or territorials. Our parents warned us not to go out with 'those soldiers'. We had been brought up to respect our parents and took their advice seriously but, looking back now,

23

I feel it was sad that this attitude prevailed. Needless to say, many of my friends eventually met their future husbands through Weybourne Camp and we did get invited to their At Home days.

In the days leading up to the Second World War, there was much talk about Hitler and Mussolini, whom we all treated as a joke. When we did go to the cinema, sitting all together in a row, as soon as Mussolini came on the screen with his large body, arms akimbo, gesticulating and roaring, we would burst out laughing, the boys with us would roll about with glee. But we sobered up a bit when the Italian Army overran Abyssinia.

We saw newsreels showing us the Maginot Line and the Siegfried Line, and the news announcer would tell all and sundry that nothing would ever get past the Maginot Line. Our boys would be just as positive, so as soon as Adolf Hitler's face appeared there would be more laughter as he strutted about at all the rallies in Germany. No one took him seriously; it was all a great big joke.

One evening, we heard there was to be a political meeting at the corner of Augusta Street, so we decided to go along. When we got there a few of the local 'blackshirts' were waiting there, all dressed up in their uniforms. We had heard about these local men but had not really believed what we had heard and treated them as a joke too, but there they were. Soon three men appeared and boxes were placed for them to stand on - it turned out to be Oswald Moseley and his henchmen. I remember nothing of what was said - after all, we were young and thought it all a game.

The months and years that followed were far from a game.

Chapter 4. Gathering Clouds

Having little means of transport out of town, most of our pleasure and relaxation was within a few miles. Chiefly we would walk along the promenade from end to end, passing others on the same occupation. We never seemed to tire of this and would traverse the length of the promenade several times, occasionally making a détour round the town centre. When the bridge was built over the West End gangway, we had a short cut to the West promenade.

My immediate friends, ten young women all about the same age, were Renée Hannah who lived in the little house near the Town Clock (which still stands today), Joan Graver whose father had a taxi-cab business, and Edna Hardingham, Peggy and Betty Farrow (Lobster family), Barbara and Joan Sadler, Phyllis Chastney and one or two others. We always enjoyed each other's company and if there was some kind of enjoyment to be had we were sure to be there. We always tried to give birthday presents and, as we had very little money to spare, we contributed 6d. each to buy a small birthday gift.

Well, 1938 was to be an eventful year for me as I would be celebrating my 21st birthday in May. Celebrating one's birthday in those days was quite often disappointing. I sometimes got a present from my sister and something to wear from my mother, so I was very pleased to get a small gift from my friends. The week before my birthday I had been rather unwell and some nasty places appeared on my neck and chin. The doctor said it was probably the north wind and dismissed it as trivial. As I had lived on the edge of the North Sea for twenty years Mother was not impressed. 'Well that takes the cake,' she said, 'I've never heard such squit!' So we went back to using some old home-made remedies.

We had all planned to go to the fair on Beeston Common on the night of my birthday, Saturday 15th May. Bert Woodrow and the Holt boys were coming over too, so this was something we were looking forward to. All that week I was quite concerned about the red, scaly places appearing; they certainly weren't getting better and I was feeling jaded too. I went to bed on the Friday night, feeling quite unwell, and on the following morning I felt very ill indeed. When my mother came into my bedroom she was shocked at the sight of me; I never saw myself in the mirror that day, but from her reaction I must have looked awful. I could hardly open my eyes, my head felt like lead, and I felt my face and I knew that there were far more places on my face and neck. My Mother ran round to her next-door neighbour, Hannah Mary Middleton, who dashed up the stairs and looked at me in horror, saying, 'Oh Mary Anne, you must get the doctor to her straight away, she looks as if she has been poisoned.'

Doctor Beaton arrived almost immediately. He took a good look at me, took my temperature and asked me where I worked and what my job was. He told my mother I was very ill and he pronounced it to be dermatitis, probably picked up at work. So my 21st birthday was spent in bed and I could only imagine my friends all enjoying themselves at the fair.

My illness developed very quickly; my arms were covered in angry red, scaly places, and so also were my fingers, neck, head and face. The doctor prescribed some ointment, which was put on all these places by my mother. I was never shown the mirror, in fact it was kept out of sight.

The next two weeks I remained in my bedroom and in bed, I gradually began to feel a bit better after about two or three weeks. Dr Beaton had called in every day and was pleased with the progress I had made. He now said 'I want you to go out into the air as soon as you feel able to. When I demurred he continued, 'Once you go out, the air will help these patches to go. You will find that the scaly places will fall off.'

I wasn't too keen on this and dreaded meeting anyone, but Mother wisely took me up Cremer Street, saying, 'We will go all round the alleyways. No one will be about at dinner time.' She was absolutely right as usual and it was amazing how the dry skin and scales just fell off and I soon got a soft new skin in its place. It was a blessing to feel better again and able to see my friends. One evening, many days after my birthday, they all appeared, bringing me a box of chocolates and all the usual girlish gossip. According to them I'd got to hurry up and get well as there were two sailors on leave in the town, I suppose the appearance of these smart fellows, after the usual khaki-clad figures, was most exciting.

I wasn't that impressed. I was quite happy taking my dog Prince out, but they continued to say that one of them, Charlie

Wright, and his mate Stanley had been on the China station for two and a half years, serving on H.M.S. *Duchess* and Charlie possessed a motor-bike. One evening, as we assembled on the sea wall, away came the two fellows looking exceedingly smart in their uniforms and I was duly introduced.

A very smart wedding was to take place at Upper Sheringham Church on Saturday the 18th June. Valerie Mansfield, daughter of Lord and Lady Sandhurst, was being married to Viscount Parker. A large marquee was to be put up in the park and fishermen were to provide a guard of honour at the church door using the lifeboat oars of the *Henry Ramey Upcher*. My father, Henry William West ('Joyful') was among those that were chosen, and it was to be a grand occasion. The womenfolk of the fishermen were invited to the reception and they were all looking forward to the event. On the Friday evening, June 17th, my friend Renée and I thought we would go along to watch them rehearsing in front of the Ramey shed.

That afternoon I remember taking my dog for a long walk through the woods; it was lovely summer weather, and I little realized what a fateful day this was to be. In the evening Renée and I collected with the others to watch the fishermen with their oars. Quite a crowd was there and the rehearsal was hilarious, for although these fishermen could control and manoeuvre their oars at sea in all weathers, they were making a right fist of it, waving them around, some up, some down, if two got it right there would be four or five getting it wrong. At last, with several orders and commands from the deputy launching officer, the drill was beginning to look passable, and finally it was agreed that everything would be 'all right on the great day'. After this, they all went off to the nearest pub to quench their thirst.

Renée and I, having enjoyed a good laugh, went off along the promenade towards the East End beach. As we got near to the tank shelter, just ahead of us were two smartly-dressed sailors, going in the same direction. Rather impetuously, as we got along-side them, I touched the collar of one of the sailors saying, 'Touch your collar for luck!' To my great dismay and surprise when he turned round to look at me it was not the person I expected. Here was a complete stranger and I apologized profusely, feeling quite an idiot. They then walked on and Renée and I joined my mother and a friend.

27

Next day, Saturday, was Aldborough Fair day and most of my friends were going. Aldborough Fair was a great local occasion but I never managed to get there. In the evening of that day as we stood near the sea wall, some of my friends were going off, leaving Renée and I to pass our time in Sheringham. Then a motor-cycle appeared and on it were two sailors. One was Charlie Wright of Weybourne, and the one on the back was the sailor whose collar I had touched the previous day. I was then introduced to Bill Ayers from Lowestoft, who had been on the China station for two years. This was my first meeting with the man I was to marry, although I didn't realize it then.

Over the few days that he was staying with Charlie at Weybourne it was inevitable that we should come into contact. He had joined the Royal Navy at the age of fifteen and had been on H.M.S. *Duchess* at Hong Kong.

Although we all tried to enjoy our days and evenings these were troublesome times. I suppose, being young, we put quite a lot of the news we heard from radio and newspapers to the back of our minds, but the threat of war was always with us. During 1936 and 1937, when each month we heard that the German troops were massing on the borders of the Sudetenland, Austria, and Czechoslovakia, we were inclined to think it would all blow over. Now this didn't seem so likely.

However, we continued attending the Aysgarth Hotel in South Street for sporting activities with the Junior Imperial League; we would go over to the Cromer pier Rollerdrome costing about sixpence, plus a few pence for hire of the skates. We also frequented Sheringham's 'Casino' (not a real Casino of course) where we spent our time playing simple card games, drinking cups of tea and coffee, playing the fruit-machines and I believe that boys could play snooker. We also had table tennis matches; it cost very little to go there and my recollection tells me it was a large, glass-sided, wooden structure on what is now the Sea View car park.

Bill stayed in Weybourne for about three days and then had to return to his home at Lowestoft on the Wednesday. Needless to say, he came to Sheringham on that morning and we walked together along the promenade. He had to catch the train at 3.30. We all went to the station with him and I thought that would probably be the last time I should see him. Charlie Wright went with him for a few days in Lowestoft and then back to Chatham

Bill Ayers in Hong Kong, aged 18

Barracks.

Some weeks passed and then surprisingly, enclosed with a letter sent to my friend Peggy, there was a letter from Bill to say how much he had enjoyed our company and that he was coming to Norfolk again. That was the beginning of a long correspondence, carried on despite his transfers to various naval vessels.

Of course there were many times when I did not hear from him and assumed that he was not interested - after all men said things and didn't always mean them.

Our days were spent working, and leisure time consisted of visits to the cinema when we could afford it, long walks over the cliffs to Weybourne and Salthouse, through the park at Upper Sheringham accompanied by various local boys. Throughout 1938, news of German troop manoeuvres on the borders of Europe worried us now and again, but these things were quickly put to the back of our minds. Today was ours; nobody was going to spoil that. The sun shone and we were happy - we looked no further than the present.

At the same time as writing to Bill Ayers, I was writing to Bill Hood, one of the soldiers who had been at Weybourne Camp. While at Weybourne he had become friendly with Renée, but she didn't return his affection once she had met the sergeant whom she eventually married. So when Bill was drafted to the Middle East, he asked me to write to him, which I did out of sympathy; his letters were always most interesting, describing the desert regions and the traditions and customs of the area. He sent me many photos of Egypt, especially Cairo, and I wrote telling him all the news from Sheringham and England.

During August of that year, Bill Ayers wrote to say he was coming to Norfolk when his leave was due and would stay again with Charlie Wright at Weybourne, but when the time came he went to Lowestoft to see his father and relatives, so I was disappointed. Then one evening in early September, on the way to the cinema, I met Charlie and Billy, here unexpectedly on a flying visit. They were going to Lowestoft the next day then back to Chatham, so it was arranged for us all to meet on the Sunday morning. The day dawned bright and sunny and I went for my usual walk to get the Sunday papers, met them both, and walked along the prom to be greeted by a large group of fishermen who shouted out, 'Hullo, wuss the fleet in port again?' I pretended I didn't know what they were talking about, blushed crimson and walked on.

Charlie went to see Charlie Ireland, another Sheringham sailor (later to be lost at sea), leaving Bill and I to take a quiet walk on our own by Hooks Hill Road and Abbey Road. We had much in common, and it was a delightful walk for us both. It was then that I realized he meant much to me, and I hoped our friendship would continue.

Chapter 5. We are at War

All through the years of 1937 and 1938 we were aware of the possibility of war; there was crisis after crisis, but each would blow over and we would relax again.

Regular soldiers were in now in residence at Weybourne Camp and my friends got to know many of them. Some became engaged to them and others were 'going steady'. The territorials, from various parts of the country would come for a week or two to be trained on the A.A. guns. At first we were very aware of the heavy gunfire, night and day, but gradually we got used to it. Many important people visited the site and inspected the troops and guns. We heard rumours that von Ribbentrop, the German Ambassador, had visited with many of his staff. Whether these rumours were accurate was hard to tell, but my mother soon decided that they were here 'to spy out the land'.

Now and again the camp would be open to the public for their At Home days; we had to have a pass for that, but as we knew so many of the regulars it was easy to get one and very interesting to go along. We were shown all over the camp, and watched the A.A. guns being fired. There was a large cinema, dance hall and sports area and the N.A.A.F.I. for refreshments. Sometimes we walked there over the golf links or caught a convenient bus. The dances and concerts still took place in the early days of the war.

In August 1938, our Prime Minister, Neville Chamberlain, went to Germany to see Chancellor Adolf Hitler three times, and each time we hoped that peace would prevail. My friends and I would discuss the situation and what it would mean. Those who were engaged or were steadily dating their soldiers all said that if war came they would definitely get married.

My close friend, Peggy Farrow, became engaged to her young man Leslie 'Blondie' Boughen. We all went to her party. Renée met Sergeant Hughes in the same year as I met Bill. He was always very generous and took us all to the Dug Out Café at the bottom of Beach Road for coffee. This was a popular haunt of the personnel from Weybourne Camp and the boys from Holt. At one time it was an ice-cream parlour run by a Mr Woodman who was also enterprising in employing young lads to walk along the beaches selling ice-cream, chocolates and sweets.

When gas masks were issued in 1938, my friend Renée Hannah and I went to help at the Sheringham Elementary School in Cremer Street. We had to show all those who came along how to put them on. There was a good deal of laughter as some of the older men would put them on upside down or back to front. Perhaps they did this to take away the seriousness of it all. The thought of putting their babies into the special gas masks went very much against the grain with the young mums, but they had to know what to do if war came. These large articles had a window through which the baby could be seen, but the baby had to be completely enclosed and many of them objected noisily and were soon taken out.

During the summer of 1938, Bill had written to say he hoped to see me on his next leave in September, but whilst on exercises he had his fingers crushed and had to go into hospital at Portland for a small operation. It was disappointing, but he and Charlie would come later in the month. Before they could arrive, however, the situation became much worse and all military and naval personnel were recalled. I received a telegram from Bill saying he had to return to Chatham Barracks. All the territorials and regular soldiers were confined to Weybourne Camp.

By Monday the 26th September, I had heard from Bill that he had been sent to H.M.S. *Resolution* and Charlie to H.M.S. *Royal Sovereign*. The same day, Hitler announced that German troops and Panzer forces would march on Czechoslovakia on Oct 1st. Everything now seemed very serious and we listened to all broadcasts. On Tuesday 27th my friends and I went again to help at the school and afterwards we listened to Mr Chamberlain's speech. It was very sombre, and later we all adjourned to the promenade. What would happen if war were declared? The boys might be called up immediately. To cheer ourselves up, we sat in the shelter along the West Prom and had a sing-song.

The next day, Parliament was recalled and the fleet was mobilized. We went to a public meeting where we were given instructions on what to do if war was declared: how to make a gas-proof room, how to lie down, or crouch down if bombs were falling, how to protect ourselves against falling glass. We went home with a handful of instruction leaflets.

Once more Mr Chamberlain was to fly to Germany to see Hitler in the hope of preventing war in Czechoslovakia. On his return from Germany, the Prime Minister said his talks with Herr Hitler had been profitable and he waved a paper in the air as he got off the plane saying it was 'peace in our time'. There was also to be a conference at Munich to sign a pact to end wars between Germany and England. At this wonderful news, the relief was great; we felt that our Prime Minister had done all he could to avert war and, believing his words, we felt we could now live without the threat of conflict.

I regularly sent to Bill the *Pink Un*, a football paper that he much enjoyed. His ship, the battleship H.M.S. *Resolution* went to Rosyth and we hoped he would get some leave for Christmas. We exchanged photos and we planned to have part of the coming Christmas at Sheringham, but it was not to be. He had only a few days leave and went to his family in Lowestoft.

Mr and Mrs Roe now asked me to go back to work, which was a great help financially. My wages were 12 shillings. At that time, I paid my mother 5 shillings, but still managed to buy chocolates, go to the cinema, pay for the club, have my shoes soled for 9d., and pay 5d. for the occasional fare to Cromer.

The New Year, 1939, opened cold and frosty. Bill had volunteered for China's war zone and he expected to go in February; he left H.M.S. *Resolution* on the 13th January and went back to Chatham. Every letter I received said he was expecting draft leave. His chum, Charlie Wright, had suddenly been sent to H.M.S. *Eskimo* and was probably going to the Mediterranean. Bill was then sent to H.M.S. *Halcyon* and later to H.M.S. *Selkirk*, both minesweepers out at sea for trials, so it seemed that the war zone in China was off the cards for the time being. We continued our correspondence and in those days, before the war, you could read about the movements of ships in the daily papers, so I knew where he was.

By March 17th radio and newspapers were reporting further trouble in many parts of Europe. Things seemed to be getting ever more serious. The Germans marched into Moravia and Ruthenia, then Hungarian troops marched into Carpathia; daily we heard of troop movements and fighting in Hungary.

Cinema newsreels showed us these events taking place, but some of the boys we knew would calmly say, 'They'll never get

33

past the Maginot Line. They'll never do anything –it's all hot air.' Never the less we wondered.

Bill was suddenly told he was going to a new ship and joined her on 27th March. She was brand new and being commissioned, H.M.S. *Mashona*, one of the latest Tribal class destroyers, all named after various tribes. They were to play a big part in the coming war and many were to be lost through enemy action. Bill was very pleased with this new ship and proud to be one of the ship's company. He often wrote about the excellent speed they made, her up-to-the-minute armaments and her manoeuvrability. He told me in his next letter how they had gone past Sheringham at midnight. He also expected to get some leave but felt he had to go to Lowestoft to see his father, although he hoped to get to Sheringham if only for a day.

Easter weekend would soon be upon us. Mother had been quite ill with a gastric ulcer and this meant that, while working at the hairdresser's, I had been looking after meals for my father and brother at the same time. I was trying to get some spring cleaning done before my sister Ena and her husband came for the weekend. On Easter Saturday I had prepared the table for tea and had got my mother down for the first time. We were just going to sit down to our first crab of the year, when the back door suddenly opened and my close friend Peggy Farrow came rushing in saying, 'May, there's a sailor in the town with Mashona on his hat and I think he's probably looking for you.' Of course my friends were all aware of my writing to Bill, as were my parents, but as yet hadn't met him, so I said to my mother, 'May I bring him home?'

'Go and find the young man and tell him to come and have his tea with us,' she said. I ran out into the road and saw a sailor walking up Cremer Street looking at the numbers. Needless to say, it was Bill. I invited him back to mine, and he was introduced to mother and later to father and Bob. They pulled his leg and put him at ease by asking him jokingly if he had brought their bait. (Their bait merchant was in Lowestoft.)

Bill was the first young man I had taken home and he was to be the only one. He was quite at ease with them and stayed for tea. Later we went for a walk and met his chums. It was arranged that he should sleep at ours. It turned out to be a lovely weekend, the first of many; we went to the cinema, and cycled to Weybourne to meet Charlie's parents. My parents liked him a lot and when he stayed, Bill was happy to go off fishing with my father and brother and have a drink at the local. It was at this time that I decided to write to Bill Hood in Egypt to tell him that I felt I could not carry on writing to him. I received a lovely letter back.

In June of that year we received the bad news of the sinking of the submarine H.M.S. *Thetis* while she was on sea trials off Anglesey; various ships had dashed to her aid, *Mashona* being one of them along with *Eskimo*, but there was no hope for the men entombed - only four men escaped.

By this time, quite a number of my friends had got engaged, and some had married. I don't think Bill ever proposed to me; we just seemed to recognize that we would marry eventually, and one evening after lovely walk along the beach and home by the cliffs, he said very casually, 'I think we ought to get settled down before I leave the Navy.' He had to serve until 1947, but we both talked of the possibility of war and decided that if it came we would get married straight away. I was worried that my parents would not agree to this as I was the youngest of the family. Maybe they would think I had not known him long enough.

May (right) with Peggy Farrow at Weybourne

During those long summer days, we enjoyed many happy times, swimming, walking, and taking out picnics when our boyfriends were able to join us. Visitors were still coming to Sheringham, but there was an air of expectancy as the war clouds loomed. Mother had two visitors to stay, but they left hurriedly at the end of August.

Once more Bill got leave in July, and he spent some happy times at sea, fishing with Bob and father. The annual Regatta was still held and hundreds of people lined the sea wall to watch the crab-boat sailing races and the tug-of-war on the sands. A pig in a box at the end of a very well-greased pole fastened across the *Henry Ramey* Lifeboat was a great attraction, with many local men taking part. This event was often won by John Broughton, who had acquired the knack of getting to the end of the pole and releasing the poor pig.

Mother decided we had better get some thick material for blackouts. She was very lucky to get several yards quite cheaply; they had almost sold out as every housewife was doing the same. We also purchased several rolls of brown sticky paper to stick across the windows to prevent flying glass. Even as we did all these things, we still hoped that war wouldn't come.

Arriving at work one day, I found Mrs Roe sealing a room ready for a gas attack; everbody assumed that this was one of the weapons the enemy would use.

All military personnel were put on alert on August 23rd. Soldiers left Weybourne A.A. Camp for war positions. Troop movements in Germany and Poland made the situation tense over the Danzig Corridor.

On August 24th, notices were placed in the High Street explaining about air-raid warnings and the all-clear signal. Then the alarm was tried out, followed by the all-clear. The first was a series of moaning sounds, rising and falling; the all-clear was a long high note, in the same tone. On the same day, the Prime Minister made a speech in Parliament lasting 32 minutes; Lord Halifax also broadcast, and the Pope spoke from the Vatican. Everything, we were told, was now entirely in Hitler's hands; his actions would decide whether it would be war or peace. The situation was now very serious. Lord Neville Henderson, the Foreign Secretary flew to Berlin on 28th August, and we heard that the Mediterranean and the Baltic were closed to our shipping.

September 1st dawned a lovely summer's day. Everywhere was peaceful and beautiful; it hardly seemed possible that the world was now to be thrust into conflict. Germany had invaded Poland at 5.45 a.m. and eight towns had been bombed.

Soldiers were ready to leave, wearing tin hats and uniforms; the town was blacked out at sunset. On the Saturday the Government sent an ultimatum to Hitler, asking him to withdraw his forces from Poland. We all awaited the news from Germany, and knew that by Sunday morning at 11 a.m., if Germany did not comply with the British and French demands, war would be declared.

On the Sunday morning, 3rd September, Renée and I went to St Peter's Church where the mood was very sombre. At 11 o'clock the Reverend Grafton Guinness left the pulpit to go into the vestry, then he quietly walked backed into the church to tell us all we were now at war with Germany. Prayers were said and a hymn for peace was sung.

Outside in the brilliant sunshine, Renée and I walked quietly down Church Street, making our way to the sea wall. We knew some of our friends would be there, and as we got together we voiced our thoughts. Where would we be when the war ended? Would we see each other again?

From the west there suddenly appeared a naval vessel, H30, racing very fast and very close in. At the same time the sirens sounded. It was a terrible feeling - none of us knew what we should do. Were the Germans going to bomb us straight away? We all scattered, some going one way and some another, hiding behind walls, then the all-clear sounded and we came out from our hiding places looking rather sheepish. We were at war!

Chapter 6. Difficult Days

On Monday 4th September it occurred to us that we would need torches, batteries, candles and matches, but everyone else had thought the same. In Starlings and other shops, we were told they were sold out, and blackout material was in short supply. We felt fortunate to have bought our material when we did.

Now we had to get used to the blackout and winter was approaching. No chink of light was to be shown anywhere. At first the blackout was a nuisance, but strangely, we did get used to it. Some nights would be inky black and nothing could be distinguished, not even the roof-tops or walls - it was just complete blackness. On other evenings you could see by the light from a star-filled sky; a full moon would make us nervous when enemy planes were about.

It took some time to make the blackout curtains and stick paper across the windows. It wasn't long before my brother decided he would make some light wooden panels that could be taken out at daylight.

We saw plenty of aircraft flying low over the town in those early days; many had swastikas on, although they didn't drop any bombs then. No doubt they were doing a reconnaissance of the coast. We listened every day to the radio and also tuned into the light vessels. In those early days of the war we could stand on the sea wall and watch convoys of ships going past, usually with three or four destroyers. One evening we counted forty vessels. They came in very close in the early days, but after a time mines were laid and the convoys kept further out.

In the early days of the war when our troops were across the channel, large maps of Europe were printed as supplements in the daily papers. Mother kept these and put them on the living room wall. With the maps were small flags, British, French and German. At first we didn't use them, but as events became more serious they became very handy and caused many lively discussions between my parents.

Mother liked to tune in to the radio, hoping to pick up Lord Haw Haw. He would be spewing out propaganda over the airwaves and often reported ships being sunk before we got the news. Sometimes he proved to be accurate, sometimes not, but it was fascinating to listen to him as he articulated in a pronounced 'posh' accent. My father hated him and would not tolerate us listening to him. If he happened to hear us listening in, he would shout 'Put that old b..... off! I won't listen to such rubbish, and don't let me catch you at it again.' So we only listened when Father was out.

Dad was very patriotic and was adamant that we were never going to lose the war, no *never*, so we dare not let him know when Haw Haw had been on, or what he had said. Many ships were lost in those early days and the liner *Athenia* was torpedoed on the Monday following the declaration of war.

One of the first letters from Bill was heavily censored; quite large pieces had been cut out, and this carried on throughout the war. My job at Mr Roe's now ended for a second time. I was very disappointed, but they felt they could manage with only the general help, Doris Hack. Doris and I had been good friends since our days working together at Brenner's Bazaar; now I had to look for another situation.

Renée and I went up to the school to help with the evacuees that were arriving. Those people who had sufficient room were expected to take some, but we didn't have room and neither had Renée's family, so we helped the staff at the school to take some of the little ones to where they had been billeted.

Photo: H.H. Tansley supplied by Sheringham Museum

Evacuees in Sheringham, 1940

Two little girls had been allocated to go to Charlie Wright's mother at Weybourne. We knew they would have a happy home there with lots of love and care, but the little sisters found it hard to settle. Mrs Wright said they would not sleep in a bed, only underneath it, and they would only eat such things as baked beans, because they were used to eating out of a tin. However, evacuation to Sheringham was soon seen to be a bad idea and a great many of the children were sent to towns further away from the coast. Some went to Cresswell in Staffordshire.

We constantly heard of mines being sighted off the shore, making it necessary for the promenade to be roped off. Once a lifeboat was washed ashore from a ship that had been sunk. Incidents occurred all along the coast, and lifeboats were frequently launched.

Suddenly, early in the morning of 26th October, Dad came to my bedroom door and called to say Bill was home on leave, it was a lovely surprise and very unexpected. His ship was in for repairs, and he had seven days leave. This became the norm as the war progressed, never knowing where they were and constantly wondering, then suddenly he would be home on leave. It seemed quite natural to us that he came to regard Sheringham as home, for although he had relatives at Lowestoft, his parents were separated and he felt far more at home with us.

It proved to be a very happy weekend. Father, Bill and I were invited to tea at Weybourne Mill, owned by Mr Dodds (see *Memoirs of a Shannock*), and we discussed getting married. I was sure my parents wouldn't agree to this, but we thought we would ask them. Surprisingly, they said that if we were happy and sure about it, they could see no reason why not. I'm sure Bill thought we could do this quite easily, but I explained it meant being in church to hear our banns called three times first, and the difficulty of this was he could never be sure when he would get leave. Everything depended on the war and where his ship was and when it would be in port.

From then on, Mother and I began putting on one side the ingredients for our wedding cake. My sister had just bought me a very pretty two piece in a lovely shade of blue, so this was put on one side. A blouse was bought, and shoes, coat and hat. There were very few white weddings in those early days of the war; there was no money to spare for luxuries. We all thought it would look rather bad to make a great show when men and women were going off to fight for the country. Just so long as we could get married quietly that was all we needed.

Bill's two friends, Charlie Wright and Stan Holman were courting and talking of marriage too. Charlie asked me to help him choose a wedding ring and we went along to Hughes & Bailey's, the jewellers in Church Street. This certainly seemed strange, but then everything was strange in those days; once the war began, nothing was the same.

Soldiers were billeted all over the town in the hotels, such as the Sheringham Hotel, the Grand and the Burlington. Boarding houses were requisitioned and several large houses taken over by the military. We got to know quite a few at the early part of the war; the Cambidgeshires were here and they were followed by the Leicesters. Canteens were established in the town for the troops and my friends and I served in them in the evening. There was one in Station Road, run by the ladies of the Methodist Chapel, who were always extremely busy making soup, beans on toast, chips and the usual. I helped there with Hannah Mary Middleton, our next-door neighbour. Another one, for ex-servicemen, was up a flight of stairs that led from Bertram Watts' shop in Church Street. Darts, dominoes, cards and food were available and soldiers were made very welcome. I also worked at the canteen in the Sheringham Hotel. Bill was concerned that I had to walk a long way home in the dark, but most of the others were the same and we all walked home together.

On 14th October Haw Haw told his listeners that H.M.S. *Royal Oak* had been sunk by a U-Boat which had got into Scapa Flow. This was denied by our Government at first but then announced on 17th October.

Stanley Holman's aunt and uncle, Mr and Mrs Harry Rix, lived in a small bungalow in Beeston Road. This kind couple had no children of their own and doted on their nephew and on Bill. I often went to see them, and remember the many photos in their living room showing Stan's friends, all sailors in uniform, Charlie, Bill, and many of Stanley and their other nephews. When I met Mrs Rix in the town, she would always ask after them and tell me her latest news of Stan. Then one day she told me that Stan and Flo were to be married, possibly before Christmas. Flo was a quiet girl, but very nice, and they seemed well suited.

On the night of Dec 6th, we were all in bed when I heard a plane flying very low and making intermittent spluttering noises. Then there was a banging on the front door; it was Henry Downtide West calling up my father and shouting loudly, 'Lifeboat!'. It had been arranged that men would be called up if needed rather than use the usual maroons. I immediately called my father and dressed hurriedly in plenty of warm clothes as it was a stormy night. There was a strong northerly wind and pouring rain as we ran down the road towards the promenade. Dad told me to go back, but I disregarded this and carried on running, he was quite angry with me, saying, 'There could be Germans about, you'll have to go back home,' but we met others running too, all of us in complete blackout, blundering along, feeling our way by the walls and alleyways.

When we got near to the lifeboat shed, many others had already gathered. We got down the steps to the beach and the sea was extremely rough, the waves breaking and bringing ashore an aeroplane. At first we were not sure what sort of plane it was, but there, clear enough for us all to see in the torch-light, was the swastika, and hanging in the cockpit was a pair of binoculars. Men with ropes dashed down towards the wreckage and managed to get it fastened to the breakwater. The lifeboat was launched for a search and some wreckage was found. (See *Memoirs of a Shannock*).

The following morning, quite early, we set out along the promenade again. Scores of people were going along the sand as the tide was now out, so Father and I joined them, making our way to the wrecked plane. Soon we were stopped by troops as the plane had been roped off; naval guards were everywhere, on the beach, on the promenade and on top of the cliffs. On all the placards around town were the words, 'German plane brought down by secret weapon.' The papers were full of pictures and far-fetched stories, but we did learn that the plane was a Heinkel 115 minelaying aircraft. (Se front cover) A few days later, the bodies of the two Germans were washed ashore; they were given a military funeral at the cemetery along the Weybourne Road.

My father had heard that the airmen were to be buried on 23rd December. The weather had turned very cold and everywhere was white with snow when I took myself along the Weybourne Road. It was just noon and hardly anyone was there. I stood quietly at the side of the hedge on the east side of the cemetery. When the hearse arrived, along with a firing party from the R.A.F., a German flag, red, yellow and black with the swastika, covered the coffins and a salute was fired, a solemn occasion in the biting wind. After the war these two men and others were transferred to the German Military cemetery at Cannock Chase, Staffordshire.

Photo: H.H. Tansley supplied by Sheringham Museum

Military honours for the German airmen, 23rd December 1939

We were constantly hearing of incidents and battles at sea. Ships of various countries were being mined along our coasts and the crews were often saved by the lifeboats from Cromer and Sheringham.

During December that year, 1939, we listened earnestly to the radio reports of the battle between the cruisers *Ajax, Achilles* and *Exeter* and the German battleship *Graf Spey*, and its flight into Monte Video harbour. There was no way of knowing where Bill's ship was or whether it was involved, but weeks later we would see actual scenes on the newsreels at the cinema. All places of entertainment were closed down at the start of the war; but things gradually relaxed and the cinemas and theatres opened once again. People enjoyed their visits to the theatre, and both cinemas in the town showed films and newsreels twice nightly, first house at 5.30 p.m. or 6 o'clock, last house at 8.15 p.m. The picture houses were always packed, and if an alarm sounded while we were in the cinema, it would be flashed on the screen so that we could choose what to do, leave or stay in our seats. At first people fled quite quickly, but after a while people relaxed and stayed to enjoy the film. Sometimes one would get several alarms in one evening.

The weather set in very bad towards the end of 1939. At Christmas it became very cold. Hail and sleet came on the 27th to be followed by several inches of snow. I heard that Stan Holman was coming home on leave on the 28th, to be married to Flo on the Saturday, so I hurriedly decided to buy a wedding present for them from Bill and I, and managed to get a nice clock.

Men aged 23-27 were being called up now and several of our friends, Sheringham lads, were now in the Army, R.A.F. or Navy. Quite a number of the Sheringham men went into the Navy on minesweepers or coastal patrol vessels, in all branches of the service. They were to go to all parts of the war zone, and many of us, left behind at home, decided to keep in touch with them all by letter with photos and news.

Despite the grim situation, there were opportunities for relaxation. The old cinema on the Cromer Road became a concert hall, and the Grand and Sheringham Hotels opened up their ballrooms for dances and N.A.F.F.I. concerts, which only cost 9d. and were really good fun. A Carnival Dance or a Barn Dance would be held on special nights; the floor would be crowded and there were always plenty of partners. I never saw any bad behaviour. There were the Military Police to keep a watchful eye out, but I never saw a fight or heard about any riots.

Chapter 7. 1940 And all That

The year came in with the worst weather we had suffered for many years. Over the Christmas period we had freezing conditions with snow squalls. These became more frequent and snow covered the roads making it hard to get about.

On Wednesday the 3rd January I had an invitation to tea at Mrs Rix's as Stanley and Flo were staying there that weekend. We were chatting together, keeping ourselves warm by the fireside, when suddenly there was a knock at the outside door and Mrs Rix called my brother in to explain that a telegram had arrived from Bill. 'Coming home 19th January, make all arrangements for wedding.' A few days later I walked through the snow to see the Reverend Grafton Guinness at the Vicarage.

In those days, the Vicarage was on Hooks Hill Road, quite a long way from my house, but I arrived there only to be told that we would need a special licence to be married as there would not be three clear Sundays for the banns to be called. This meant I had to write a letter to Holt or to the Cathedral in Norwich. I was surprised a few days later when a friend, Nelly Grice, told me she had been at St Peter's Church on Sunday the 7th and heard my banns called. Then a letter arrived saying a special licence was at the Reverend King's for me to collect.

I took the train to Holt, which was quite easy then, as the line ran through to Melton Constable, and beyond to the Midlands and the North. The countryside looked beautiful in the snow and I met the Reverend King at Holt Church and purchased the special licence for £2 6 s. We could now get married on what ever day we wished, for there was always the possibility that Bill's leave would be cancelled.

On Sunday January 14th there were heavy falls of snow all over the area, the worst weather experienced for many years. Many villages were cut off and snow ploughs were out to clear some roads. The following Saturday we expected Bill, but he didn't arrive. Charlie called round and we set off for the station to meet the 2.30 train but he wasn't on it. When we got back to the house, however, a telegram was there saying that he was arriving the next day.

Charlie took me to Hughes & Bailey's in Church Street to buy us a wedding present, and I decided to have some cutlery, a nice gift for us. More snow fell that weekend and roads were very bad, Bill had to get a taxi at Cromer to get him home by 3 o'clock in the afternoon. The next day we walked through thick snow to the Vicarage and arranged our wedding for Wednesday 24th January. We hurriedly visited our friends and relations to invite them to come and share our day. Peggy Farrow was going to be my matron of honour. Charlie, Bill and I went to shop for white ribbon for their uniforms, ordered flowers and booked cars and then went to Hughes & Bailey's to buy our wedding ring.

Our wedding day dawned fine and the sun shone. The ceremony such as it was, was at 9 o'clock and there were not many people about. The roads were covered with snow and ice, and teams of men were out clearing the streets. My brother was employed by the Council, in charge of several men and their shovels, so he wasn't going to be at the church.

I wore the blue bouclé two-piece with a white blouse and a spray of orange blossom and white heather. Bill and Charlie, his best man, were in naval uniform. My father was to give me away and he was soon smartly dressed. It was a solemn occasion in the Church, but many of my friends and relatives were there in festive mood to share our day back home. The little house was soon full. Presents and telegrams kept arriving - things seemed to be far more prompt and regular in those wartime days, despite all the chaos and difficulties.

A good crowd assembled indoors for drinks, eats and wedding cake. Then my brother Bob brought in a whole load of chaps and someone began cutting them huge slices of cake. I could hardly believe my eyes. This was the cake we had collected all our rations for! I couldn't see it going very far at that rate. Luckily, I did manage to retrieve portions to send to friends and relatives, especially my sister Ena and her husband. The day was such a whirl of enjoyment and excitement that I don't think I ever got a taste of the cake.

At 12 noon we had to leave for the station to have our honeymoon at my sister's near Luton. What a place to chose for a honeymoon! But it was where Ena and Don lived. Nearly all of the company decided to come to the station and give us a send-off. Special messages and kind words were said and I noticed Father taking Bill on one side and giving him some words of advice. After all I was the baby of the family and Dad no doubt thought it was important.

At Luton Hoo we had to change trains, and when we got out of the train there was total darkness, not a light to be seen anywhere. Carrying the suitcase, which was fairly heavy, we groped our way along the platform, having no idea where anything was. We opened one door very tentatively so as not let out any ray of light, and pulled back a dark grey blanket to see five or six men sitting round a stove. They looked at us in astonishment and tried to direct us to the correct platform. Out in the dark again, we groped our way and found a seat. At last our train arrived and we got on board; there was no light at all to see if this was the correct one, but once on board the guard grunted, 'Yus, two more stops, then Luton'.

We had not realized just how far it was from Luton Station to my sister's home. The snow was deep everywhere and an icy wind was blowing. We set out on foot, hoping to see a bus or someone to ask, but it was 8.30 and no one was about anywhere. After a couple of miles, Bill said, 'Whatever have you put in this suitcase? I bet there's enough in here to last a month and we're only going for a couple of days.' Although he had been quite happy to fall in with my wish to go to Ena's, I think he was already looking forward to being back in dear old Sheringham.

On honeymoon at Stopsley

47

Suddenly, a bus came very slowly along the ice-packed road and we were able to get to Stopsley where Ena had a lovely meal for us and we could enjoy the warmth of the fireside. We spent the rest of the evening reminiscing and reporting about the events and happenings of the past few days.

The next day Ena went with us on the bus into town, she wanted to buy us a nice dinner service as their wedding gift to us. We chose a nice one with a green border on a cream background. In those few days we also managed to get to the theatre to see Troise and his Mandoliers.

January continued the same with very heavy falls of snow and freezing temperatures. On February 2nd, just as Bill's leave was ending, a telegram came saying he had got a further seven days leave. It was a wonderful surprise as I dreaded his return to his ship, not knowing when we would see each other again. He never made any comment about going back but he was quiet and subdued.

About this time we heard of ships and lightships being attacked by Nazi planes. We often heard of these attacks by tuning our radio to the marine band. On 9th February, 1940, we heard the East Dudgeon lightship calling. The Sheringham and Cromer for assistance but felt helpless. We could only hope that the lifeboats would get there in time.

Another time *Yarmouth Coaster* was attacked and our lifeboat went to her aid. Father, Bill, Mother and I went as far the lifeboat shed to see her arrive home safe with seven men on board, some injured by machine-gun bullets.

During the war years, leave arrangements for service men and women were very erratic. Sometimes they would get home, only to be recalled immediately. At other times their leave would be prolonged. Often Bill went back and we had a sad parting only to have him walk back in unexpectedly. When coming home late at night Bill would often leave the train at Norwich and walk the entire way home by road in the blackout. He could never get home quick enough. When he got to Aylsham a friendly nightwatchman would give him a hot cup of tea or coffee.

Throughout the war, for six long years, this was the pattern. Gradually men and women were being called into the services or munitions factories, or other services like the Land Army, or the Medical Corps. We never knew when those who were away would

48

**The crew of the Foresters Centenary, Sheringham's lifeboat
from 1936-1961**
*The Foresters Centenary had a magnificent record during those years,
Thirty-four launches were associated with aircraft and their crews. Sixteen
airmen were saved.
Left to right: 'Corporal' Grice, Jimmy Scotter, Signalman Henry Little,
'Demon' Cooper, Bennet Middleton, 'Sparrow' Hardingham, Coxswain
Jimmy Dumble, Teddy 'Lux' Craske, Henry 'Downtide' West.*

be home again, if ever. I kept in touch with many of the local lads
if I could, wherever they were. They longed for letters and parcels
from home.

Practically every day there were happenings at sea, and rafts
would be sited and many large ships' lifeboats would be washed
ashore. We went down to the Lifeboat House almost every day. By
now the promenade was out of bounds and large rolls of barbed
wire were fixed all along the promenade. Tank traps were built in
several places, at Beach Road near the Station, and near the
railway lines. If we wanted to get down to the Lifeboat Station we
went around to the Marble arch and at certain places we were
allowed through. There were soldiers on guard everywhere. The
fishermen and lifeboat crew were always allowed along there, but
there were many times when we were stopped.

Bill's ship had been in for repairs and he was able to get home again on leave, going back on the 25th February. We didn't know it at the time but we were not to see each other again until the 29th June, and a great deal had taken place in the meantime.

Abroad, the war had intensified. At home, the cold freezing weather with much snow lasted right through until March.

One evening when I came in from a walk with Prince, Mother had been twiddling the knobs on the radio and had heard Lord Haw Haw report that H.M.S. *Eskimo* had been badly damaged at Narvik. This worried me a great deal as Bill's ship *Mashona* was also a Tribal class destroyer and was in the same flotilla, but it was no good thinking the worst. I learned later that *Mashona* had been diverted to Trondheim and Namsos. Patrols had been sent ashore and there were several skirmishes, with some casualties. Bill told me he had seen these Norwegian towns ablaze, but some Nazis were captured and brought back to England.

On the morning of Tuesday April 9th we were told that the Germans had taken Denmark and had invaded Norway. The following day there was news of battles taking place along the Norwegian coast near Bergen, and Narvik. Many of our destroyers had been involved with considerable damage being done. Winston Churchill spoke to us on the radio, and over the coming terrible months he was to hold the attention of the nation in his expressive way. He didn't try to pull the wool over our eyes, but his patriotic fervour instilled in all of us a feeling that we *must* win through. Whenever he was going to speak on the wireless the whole population waited with baited breath and we would huddle around the set, listening to every word. He gave us the truth in very plain words, but then ended his speech with rousing words. When he mentioned Adolf Hitler or the Nazis he would almost bite out the words and snarl and roar like a bulldog.

We heard that *Renown* and *Rodney* had been in action; both *Ghurka* and *Glow-worm* had been lost. By this time I was very worried, but I tried to put it at the back of my mind. Then a letter came from Bill, but it had been posted some time before. The Admiralty announced that many of our ships had entered the Fiord and attacked Narvik, seven German ships had been sunk, three of ours damaged and *Eskimo* badly damaged with many injured.

During the Easter period, I stayed a week with friends at

Dovercourt, and one night we heard a massive explosion and much gunfire. Later we heard that a bomber had crashed at Clacton with five people killed and 90 injured. This was in the Harwich and Parkestone Quay area with lots of naval personnel and plenty of warships in the estuary. Some of our ships had been sunk by magnetic mines, which German planes had laid in those waters.

On the morning of May 10th we awoke to the horrifying news over the radio that the Nazis had invaded Holland and Belgium. At 3 am Amsterdam and Brussels had been bombed with heavy loss of life. The German Panzers had swept forward so quickly that by the 14th May Holland had surrendered to the Germans. We were told that 100,000 men were killed at Sedan, and on Belgian/ French soil. The British Expeditionary Force was in action and the Navy was also active along the coast.

The maps we had from the early papers were now coming into daily use. Mother had pinned a very large one of the Low Countries, France and Belgium on the wall and with tiny flags of the countries involved, we were able to pin these flags where the actions were. The radio was almost constantly giving out details and it was frightening to see the speedy advance of the German army with their tanks and Panzer troops, surrounding towns in the north of France and towards the coast. One night I remember we had been discussing this advance, and Mother was moving the little British flags. 'Look at this!' she said, pointing to the area of the Maginot Line. 'Look where they are now, they're going to trap our men.'

Father, very annoyed, got up out of his elbow chair and went across the room to look closely at the map. 'Ha!' he said. 'This is all right. This is just what *we* (meaning the Allies) want. We shall trap them all there. Look at where our forces are, and *there's* the Maginot Line. They can't get past that - this is just what we want, you'll see.'

Ever the same spirit - we were always going to win - but the next day the Nazis had surged ahead and our men were trapped in pockets along the coast at Dunkirk where the B.E.F. was now in extreme danger.

On Saturday May 25th, the Germans were near Calais and Boulogne and there were more heavy losses. The next day, Sunday, was a day of national prayer all over the country. Many thousands of people went to churches throughout the land to pray

51

for the men and for our country. I went to St Peter's that evening with friends. On Tuesday we had more bad news. The King of the Belgians had capitulated and left our men surrounded on all sides. Destroyers shelled Boulogne while our troops were being brought back to England. Winston Churchill spoke in Parliament; things were grim indeed.

Father came home to say that all boats available must go to the help of the men stranded on the beaches at Dunkirk, and on the 30th May I stood, with many others, on the sea wall to watch the departure of the boats that were big enough to go. It was a lovely calm evening, warm and sunny. The *Liberty,* with Billy 'Cutty' Craske and his son, Teddy, Young 'Downtide' West and Jimmy Bishop, was followed by *Edna* crewed by Fred 'Dingy' Middleton, 'Kiff' Pegg and Walter 'Tooshy' Brown. These two were escorted by a few others to bid them 'God speed'; it was a touching sight. We learned later that they reached Ramsgate but were not allowed to go across to Dunkirk.

When Father came home after seeing them go he was most concerned about 'Tooshy', saying, 'I think he must be crazy. He's now gone there, leaving his wife Evelyn and all her children.' But that was the usual way with Walter; he thought nothing of danger, he just had to go. Thankfully they all returned home safely.

By this time Neville Chamberlain had resigned and Winston Churchill had become Prime Minister to take us through the darkest days. We heard and remembered his famous words, 'We shall fight them in the fields, we shall fight them on the landing grounds, we shall fight them on the beaches. We will *never surrender.'*

By June 14th Paris had fallen into enemy hands and Mussolini had declared war on us. The Italians were crossing the southern border of France, Germany now occupied the Netherlands, Norway and Denmark and nearly all of France was in enemy hands. By 17th June Britain was left fighting alone. The German troops were only just across the Channel, a matter of twenty odd miles away. If Hitler could overrun those other countries, what could he do to us? How soon would he order his forces to invade our land?

Chapter 8. Into the Conflict

The country was informed that church bells would be rung all over the land if invasion came. We expected this hourly but everybody went about the daily routine as usual. We had to carry our identity cards wherever we went. There was also a curfew and people were told to be in their homes by nine o'clock in the evening. I remember visiting my friends in Common Lane on those summer nights but leaving each time by a quarter to nine. Sentries were everywhere and you were often challenged by members of the military on guard duty. Very few people were about the town in the evening; most people would stay near to their radios.

There were rumours in the town of spies and aliens along the coast. We heard that quite a well-known family in Cliff Road had been taken away. With so many rumours, we dare not discuss them or believe them. Holiday visitors to the town had ceased to come, so the beaches were completely empty. We could still make our way to the beach when the weather was fine, but gradually places became out of bounds. Beeston Hill became a site for artillery and the A.T.S., soon to be fenced off with barbed wire, Ack Ack guns and military on patrol. The golf course too was fortified with naval guns on Skelding Hill and underground tunnels. The whole area was out of bounds.

The cliffs all along the coast were mined by various regiments at this time all the way along to Weybourne. We heard tales of soldiers being maimed and killed by these mines, and for many years after the war, they were still being uncovered by high tides. As those glorious summer days went slowly by, we heard of children being evacuated from the east coast as danger was imminent, and we listened to the news of the men being rescued at Dunkirk. All this time I got letters from Bill, but never knew where he was or when I should see him again.

We had constant air-raids; the alarm and all-clear were almost continuous. We did not have an air-raid shelter then, although some people had Anderson shelters in their gardens. When the alarm went at night Mother and I would get up and make a cup of tea, then go back to bed. Father would stay in bed and say, 'If it's got my name on it I might as well stay in bed.' Mother would get anxious and go to the foot of the stairs and call out 'Willie are you getting up? They (the Jerries) are right overhead.' The searchlights would be criss-crossing the sky and occasionally planes would drop a 'chandelier', a series of bright lights that hung suspended above us for what seemed ages. At moments like these I would be really afraid; the light was so bright you could read a newspaper. I really felt that the Germans could see every nook and cranny.

One time Father really did get aroused was when they were dropping incendiaries and he flew down the stairs in his nightshirt saying, 'Blast the b..... Germans!'

I worried if I did not hear from Bill, trying not to think the worst, then perhaps I would get two or three letters all at once, no postmark to identify where he was, and all heavily censored. Sometimes the letters were practically indecipherable.

One Sunday at the end of June, it had been a glorious hot day and I had walked with my dog Prince as far as Beeston. I sat in the sunshine for a while, thinking about Bill and wondering where he was. We hadn't seen each other since February, which seemed a long time ago. As I turned into the alleyway, which divided our house from our neighbour's, I heard voices and thought we had company and that it would disturb our usual Sunday teatime. When I opened the cottage door, there stood Bill, talking to Mum and Dad. He looked tired and unshaven and was wearing a very heavy home-knit sweater, suitable for wearing in arctic waters. He was explaining that he had got 48 hours leave and had come all the way from Scapa Flow. It was wonderful to see him again, even for such a short visit.

After a wash and change of gear, we had our tea and then went over the golf links as far as the end of the course. It was a glorious evening. We set out to see a few of our relations and friends and had a drink in the Windham Arms, which was crowded with soldiers. When you went into the pubs in those days, great, thick, blackout curtains would cover the doorways and it was quite a battle to get in or out. With that, and a mass of military every-where, you had to fight to get to the bar for a pint. However, the atmosphere was always friendly, jolly and nostalgic. There would be friends home on leave and friends departing after leave, a great feeling of comradeship and fighting for a cause, and of relief at being home with one's own people.

It was a short leave for Bill and I, but a very happy one. He still made time to see my grandmother 'Joyful' and Uncle John and Aunt Lizzie, my mother's brother and sister-in-law. He also went to the sea front to talk to the fishermen, but his train left at 2 o'clock and it didn't leave us much time, so I went with him on the train to Norwich, giving us just another hour or so together. He was sad at going, but we looked forward to being together again. He never spoke about his experiences at sea, just took it all as a matter of course, but we knew his heart was here in Sheringham.

About this time my friend Peggy Farrow had been planning her wedding to Leslie Boughen whom we called 'Blondie', a nice chap who was in the army. Renée and I had been invited. Peggy lived at that time with her family in New Road; the little house was crowded on the day of the wedding, 10th August. The bride was all in white and Betty, her sister, in a pink and mauve dress. It was a most enjoyable day; we stayed to tea and I gave her a table-cloth which cost 5s. 11d.

These were the days of mass air-raids on the south-east coast by Nazi planes. Our fighter planes were up all the time; it was the crisis point of the Battle of Britain. We heard of 60 and 62 enemy planes being shot down on successive days and then of 160 and 120.

Bill's ship came into Chatham and he was given ten days leave on 26th August. We went to see friends and relations and his father and sister came over from Lowestoft. He enjoyed several days fishing with my father. Mother and I went fishing with them one day and we got a good catch of mackerel, then had a great time giving them to friends. His leave was up on 4th September and he returned to Chatham. A week later all leave was cancelled as the invasion was expected.

This was a very worrying time. There were heavy raids on London with hundreds killed. Many towns were bombed constantly, yet we went ahead each day with the usual activities, working and finding time to go to the N.A.A.F.I., concerts and dances.

At one point, I decided not to go out to any entertainment because I had not heard from my husband for nearly four weeks. As the days dragged on without a letter from him, I didn't feel it was right to be enjoying myself when he could be injured somewhere or even dead. So every time my friends asked me to go

I kept saying 'No'. Then one day a letter arrived for me with large markings on that I had not seen before. I was convinced that it was something from the Admiralty telling me of the loss of Bill's ship. I wouldn't open the letter and my brother Bob was angry with me saying, 'It's from Billy. He's all right! Look, here's his signature at the corner of the envelope.' Then I too recognized his scrawl and knew he must be all right. I opened it and found it heavily censored, but I sighed with relief and made up my mind to go to the dance that evening.

The Sunday afternoon of the 22nd September was fine and warm, so Renée, Nell Spencer and I thought we would take a walk through the woods, then home to tea and St Peter's church in the evening. We enjoyed our walk but when rain fell we made for home quite early. Coming down Common Lane, (not so built up as it is now), we crossed the Cromer Road near the Beeston Road Post Office, hurrying because of the rain, and sheltered in my house in Cremer Street. Suddenly we could hear a plane flying very low. I saw both of my friends hurriedly getting under Mother's large kitchen table. I wondered why they were doing this, but decided to copy them. The plane swooped out of the clouds and dropped bombs on the area near Barford Road, causing some of the most severe blast-damage in Sheringham during the war. There was hardly a house without some sort of damage, roofs and tiles off, ceilings down, windows and doors blown off. Afterwards there were rumours that an 'aerial torpedo' had been dropped and that this was what caused the damage over such a large area.

Barford Road was evacuated. A direct hit had demolished Victoria House on the opposite corner to Beales Stores (Beeston Regis Post Office today). A lady waiting for a bus was killed and several people injured. The funny thing was my friends and I had just got our smart hats on for church and there we were scrambling under the table. When I looked at them I had to laugh at the sight, but we did not laugh for long.

We decided to go and see what damage had been done. Walking up Co-operative Street we saw windows out, glass everywhere, and fruit and vegetables rolling about in the gutters. In the High Street it was the same, clothes and hats had been blown out of shop windows, dresses and fabric everywhere. We met Mr Hannah, Renée's father who lived in the little house near the town clock. He came towards us, covered in soot and very pleased to see

Bomb damage in Cromer Road, September 1940

his daughter. He told us that part of the chimney had fallen and the ceilings were down. Needless to say, he was shaken.

After tea, like everybody else, we went to see the craters on the allotments near Barford Road, but were soon turned back by the authorities. It wasn't until the next day that we knew of the woman (Mrs Abbs) being killed. We learnt over the next week how vast the damage was.

About this time my brother Bob had to go for a medical in Norwich. He passed A1 for the Navy and hoped to get into the Coastal Patrol Service, but he would have to wait for his posting. Most of the Sheringham men had to go to the Sparrow's Nest at Lowestoft, which was the main recruitment centre for all naval personnel from Norfolk and Suffolk; some went from there to minesweepers, some to M.T.B.'s.

On October 22nd 1940 I was told of the death of young Stanley Holman, a great chum of Bill's, who had with him on the China station. I immediately wrote a letter to Bill at Chatham. It seemed he was killed when out at sea laying mines. Flo and Stan were married almost at the same time as we were, and it made me realize how vulnerable we were. I knew how distressed Flo would be, and Mr and Mrs Rix, his devoted aunt and uncle.

Bill now left H.M.S. *Mashona* and went to Chatham Barracks on a sail-maker's course, which was to take some six months. We both thought this would be an advantage when the war was over and it would mean a break between ships. The momentum of the war was increasing, so there was little chance of him staying on shore for long.

While Bill was on leave from Chatham, we heard about the loss of the *Mashona*, whilst engaged in the search for the battleship *Bismarck* in the Atlantic. Some of the crew were lost and Bill was very upset at the time. The *Mashona* lies somewhere beneath the waters of the Atlantic.

My friends and I were still helping out at the canteens in the town where we were badly needed. But now, women and girls were being called up into the forces, Land Army, Ambulance Drivers, and Red Cross. They were called up in age groups. Renée heard that she might have to go, but as she spent most of her time looking after her widowed father and as part-time assistant in the Shirley Tea Rooms in Augusta Street, that let her out.

My cousin Olive went into the W.R.N.S., which she enjoyed, and many other Sheringham girls went into the munitions factories at Luton and in the Midlands.

Christmas 1940 was a very enjoyable one. Bill got home on leave a few days before; a fire was lit in the sitting room, beautifully decorated for the festive season, and all our friends came in for games of cards. Bob still hadn't received his call-up papers and he and his pals enjoyed themselves. Then, on December 23rd, he got his papers to appear on 3rd January 1941 at Lowestoft to join the Royal Navy, It did dampen things a bit, but on the other hand we were determined to make this a great Christmas, despite the war and rationing.

Chapter 9. Set-backs and Surprises

In the face of imminent invasion the Government ordered all sign-posts to be taken down so as to confuse the enemy, but no doubt the enemy had plenty of local maps to refer to.

Holway Road in those days was heavily wooded on both sides and not as we know it today, but in 1940 one could see openings close to the ground with posts sticking out with wires attached to each one. These were cleverly camouflaged by the undergrowth. We never knew what they were for, but people remarked on them and noticed that they were also placed each side of the road near Pretty Corner and the main Cromer to Holt road. Probably they could be detonated if tanks or troops were advancing.

The government also ordered the confiscation of all iron railings or gates for the war effort. So we all lost our gates, or what-ever metal we had, to be turned into weapons. This was done quite willingly as we all felt we were playing a part.

January 1941 opened with very bad weather here on the east coast. The roads were treacherous with ice, and there were heavy falls of snow on the 17th and 18th January. Bob reported to the Royal Navy Patrol Service at Lowestoft on January 3rd. He was given his kit and billeted with fourteen other ratings in Victoria Terrace, but it was not many days before he wrote to say he was being sent to a training school at Rosyth in Scotland.

Bill came home on leave on 25th January, almost on our first wedding anniversary, but during that leave he complained of feeling unwell, suffering with stomach pains and sickness. At first the doctor said it was 'flu and he had his leave extended. He went over to Cromer Hospital a few times to see the doctors there and have X-Rays. This was the beginning of a long period of ill-health.

A ship came ashore at Sea Palling, which caused a lot of interest, and then we heard that a ship of 14,000 tons was on the Haisbro sands and Cromer lifeboat had been launched. The weather continued very bad with further heavy falls of snow in February. Inland, people were being dug out of their cottages.

We began to be concerned about Bill, who was still under the Doctor here at Sheringham. He was not at all well and the doctor wanted him to go into hospital in Norwich, as he was getting severe pains with other symptoms. He finally went into hospital for another X-Ray and I went with him. They decided not to keep him in, but a duodenal ulcer was suspected and he had to go on a strict diet. We were also told he might have to leave the Navy. Bill made no comment but didn't think leaving the service was a probability as everybody was needed. We felt lucky that they allowed him to remain here in Norfolk. During February he went backwards and forwards to Cromer Hospital or to Norwich for more X-Rays. He lost weight, and spent some time in Drayton Hospital.

We were constantly aware of gunfire from ships at sea when the 'Jerries' were over. We were out one day for a walk along Briton's Lane and then through the woods, when suddenly the A.A. guns opened fire at a German plane and some bombs were dropped on Morley Hill, but no one was hurt.

Cromer lifeboat was off several times and we heard that a large convoy had been torpedoed by E-boats. Our lifeboat was always on stand-by and the fishermen were at the lifeboat house almost hourly. In the midst of all this wartime activity, I went to see Dr Lawson and he confirmed that I was expecting our first child.

One rainy and dismal morning early in March, the sort of day when German planes were likely to do a hit-and-run raid, Mother and I decided to do our shopping, leaving Bill at home with Father repairing some crab-pots. There were quite a few people about the town on the same errands as we were. We had finished all the shopping we needed to do, and decided to make our way home by way of New Road. As we passed the Top Chapel (now gone) Mother realized that we had not bought our daily newspaper and she said 'I'd better go back to get it as Father likes his paper.' So we went back into Station Road towards the Town Clock, and as we crossed between the clock and the shops I could hear the sound of a plane in the distance. Looking up above Church Street, I could see a small speck in the sky, undoubtedly a plane, bearing towards us, and as I looked, I saw a small object leave the plane and immediately said, 'Whatever have they thrown out?' Then I came to my senses and realized it was a bomb, and that it was directed towards the town. 'Quick, Mother,' I said 'it's dropped a bomb! Quick, quick, get in somewhere!'

We were on the pavement beside Jordan's the Chemist. To the side of this was a bakery yard with a very large green door that led to Leeder's Bakery. I ran into the yard, realizing that the bomb looked like hitting the very centre of the town. Then I looked behind me - where was Mother? I had no idea where she had gone to and there was no time to go and look. All I could do was crouch down behind the large gate; the only cover, as far as I could see, was the large wall adjoining, but as I crouched there my mind was telling me that this area could receive a direct hit. There was absolutely nothing I could do. The noise of the approaching plane was loud now, and suddenly I heard the explosion of the bomb. Almost at the same time, masses of bricks came hurtling out of the sky, stones and débris all around me and being flung everywhere, hitting the walls of the confined space.

Tentatively I went to the gate and peered out, hoping to see Mother hiding somewhere. The sky above me was still full of flying débris coming from where the bomb had dropped. From where I stood, it looked as if the Robin Hood pub had been hit. By now the huge German plane was right over my head, very low, it seemed to span the space above Barclay's Bank and Leeder's Bakery. I could see every marking on it. Suddenly the bomb doors opened and out came three large bombs. They were right above me, but I wasn't at all scared of these as I could tell they were going to miss much of the town; even as they left the plane they were being carried seaward. We heard later that they had made three large craters on the water's edge.

By this time I had found Mother. She had run into the chemist's shop and, without saying anything, had got behind the counter, surrounded by glass cabinets. The assistants must have wondered whatever she was doing.

We finally got back home, minus the daily paper. Bill, very anxious, said 'Where have you been? Don't you know they have dropped some bombs? I've been worried out of my life.'

Later we heard that the bomb had made a direct hit on a house in New Street, demolishing the house where the postman Mr Hall lived. He was in bed at the time but survived the explosion. Several other houses were badly damaged in this raid of 6th March 1941.

Three days later on 9th March, which was a rainy Sunday, we were all indoors when, at about 5 o'clock, a Nazi plane swooped down, machine-gunned the town, and dropped incendiary bombs and high explosives, but no one was injured. The following day the A.A. guns drove off another enemy plane.

Bomb damage in New Street, March 1941

We were still expecting the invasion and many nights had little sleep as German planes were constantly going over. Sometimes we could hear a large 'clump' as one of the planes dropped its bomb-load out at sea.

Mother and I would get up when we heard the air-raid warnings, and one night we heard something that never was explained. We had made a cup of tea and were listening for every footfall. Sometimes we would joke and say, 'What would we do if a Jerry came to the door?' I would laugh and say, 'I'd better practice saying Heil Hitler,' just for a joke. As we sat there together we suddenly heard some strange 'swishing' noises, rather peculiar, and, as we looked at one another, there was a knock at the back door. This was about 3 o'clock in the morning and I think we both thought that the swishing noise we had heard was someone coming down on a parachute. We looked at each other wondering what to do. I grabbed a very small poker from the hearth and we opened the staircase door. Then Mother whispered to me, 'You ought to get Billy to come down and see who it is.'

I don't know what I thought I could do with that little poker, but I went to get Billy out of bed. He wasn't too pleased at being disturbed and he had heard nothing, but he came down, hastily putting on a dressing gown. He went to the door and called out into the night, 'Who's there?' There was no reply and he wasn't very long in closing and locking the door! We never heard of anyone else hearing anything but we were quite convinced that we had heard the knock.

On 24th March, Bill received a letter from Chatham informing him that he must report to hospital there for further tests prior to his discharge from the Navy. The next day he went to see relations before leaving by train. He soon settled in at Chatham.

Food was becoming ever more scarce; when you visited the local shops the shelves were nearly bare. Of course we got our ration for basic foods, but they were very small amounts. Often we would save our coupons to get some luxuries at times like Christmas or birthdays. Queues would form regularly at the shops for cakes, bread, flour, oranges, but not bananas. These were not available until after the war. People would queue for hours just to get three oranges or a tin of milk, or a jar of honey. It was the same at the butchers; meat was rationed, but offal and suet were sometimes available without coupons. The word would spread around the town quickly if a product had suddenly arrived, and you would see ladies and girls hurrying along with their pinafores on to get in a queue.

At the corner of New Road and Cremer Street, where we lived, was a very handy little shop. It had been run by Mr and Mrs Dunn, who lived nearby, but during the war it was taken over by a Mr Nelson. (This may have been his nickname; it didn't take long for a newcomer to get a nickname in Sheringham.) He was always glad of our custom and we were very glad of his merchandise. When you went to the shop, it was quite a job to get in as he had a very heavy curtain over the door. Everywhere looked dark, but once the heavy curtain was pushed aside there were empty shelves, but always a warm welcome. On the counter was a stuffed black cat, not a real one thank goodness, but one that looked quite life-like; he said it brought him luck.

We went to Mr Nelson for all manner of things, hoping to get something on the black market. We would buy our few rations and then he might suddenly put his hand down below the counter and say rather softly, 'Do you want a tin of Nestlés Milk?'

'Yes,' I would say with delight.

'Lovely!' Then up would come the tin of milk which my father would always refer to as 'dickey's milk', a firm favourite with him.

Another time it might be a tin of golden syrup. These items helped to eke out our meagre rations.

Nearly everyone trotted to Nelson's door hoping for a surprise. When sweets were rationed, we were only allowed a few ounces, so when it got near to Christmas we would go without using our coupons for many weeks, just so that we could have some extra pleasure at Christmas. I remember collecting all our coupons and then going up to his shop to spend them. What delight when he took me through to the rear premises and showed me the choice. All over the floor were cardboard boxes with toffees, bars of chocolate and all manner of goodies. I was allowed to make my choice and use all my coupons. When I see the shops today, filled with such choice and variety of goods everywhere, my mind goes back to those days of rationing and bare shelves and I think how fortunate we are.

It was a credit to the women then that they managed to feed their families, in spite of the shortages. We got tins of dried egg, a very good standby as we could do a great deal with it. Everything was 'make do and mend'. Every bit of land or garden was put to good use; allotments everywhere were willingly dug and plenty of bartering went on. Those who caught fish and had plenty to spare would exchange them for perhaps a rabbit or two.

Bill wrote to say he was being sent to another hospital but had no idea where that was to be. Then, in April, I received a letter to say he was at Aylesbury in Buckinghamshire. He had been very ill and had lost 26 lb in weight. I wrote to my sister at Stopesley asking if I could go to hers to stay as we were worried about him. Of course she wrote back to say I could go and stay as long as I liked. Within a few days I was on my way to Bedfordshire by train.

On Sunday 13th April, Ena, her husband and I went by car to see Bill at Stoke Mandeville Hospital, a very new place, catering at that time for service personnel. My sister felt that I should not go to see him alone, as she felt he was seriously ill, and I was grateful for their company.

When we arrived at the hospital and found the ward he was on, he really looked very poorly and I was upset at how he had altered. All I knew was that he was to have more X-Rays to get to the cause of the problem. Duodenal ulcers were very probable. From then on, I caught a bus to Aylesbury two or three times a week. It was a lovely journey through the Buckinghamshire countryside in the spring sunshine, going through Tring and Edelsborough. When I arrived in Aylesbury I had a very long walk to the hospital, but very pleasant.

As the days went by, Bill made some progress, but then there would be a setback. He had many tests and the doctors all said it was ulcers and put him on a strict diet. Some days, when he was well enough, we had some lovely walks in the countryside. Eventually, in June, he was allowed home on 21 days leave, looking more himself.

While staying at Ena's I often went into Luton with her to join the long queues for food. One day Ena and her friend Molly Jackson, who lived two doors away, determined to go to London, and I decided to go with them. This was the time when Rudolf Hess flew to Scotland, trying to make some sort of peace move, and everyone on the train to London was reading about him. It was headline news in all the papers. The night before there had been big raids on London, and when we walked by the Houses of Parliament the roads were littered with incendiary bombs and men were clearing up all the rubble. Inside Parliament, we could see many rooms blackened with burnt fabric and looking very desolate.

We decided to take a bus to the big stores, Selfridges, Pontings and Gamages, but got there only to find that most of their stock was below stairs in the basement. When we went down to these under-ground stores, we could see large cracks in the walls and some evidence of trickling water, a strange sight; all the stores were the same.

On the underground we could see the mattresses and belongings of those who had taken refuge there from the heavy bombing. Overhead were the silvery shapes of the barrage balloons. Many streets were full of débris, bombed out buildings and shops, but everywhere we saw the true spirit of the British people, large posters saying they were 'still in business despite Hitler and his cronies'. We couldn't help admiring the Londoners' comradeship in spite of adversity, but we were thankful to leave the great city and get back to my sister's home.

That evening we went into Mrs Jackson's for a game of cards. I turned rather faint suddenly and asked for a glass of water. Then Molly and her mother, a true Geordie, said she would tell my fortune from the cards. While shuffling the cards I dropped a few, and the old lady asked me to pick them up and show them to her face upwards. This I did and she immediately said, 'I see a blue-eyed baby boy,' and I nodded, not having told them, or my sister, that I was expecting a baby. This caused a bit of a surprise, but when we went home there were a few cross words from my sister for not telling her first.

At the end of May, Bill was discharged from Stoke Mandeville Hospital for 21 days leave. It was lovely to have him home once more and Sheringham was the place where he was happiest. Whenever he could, he went off fishing with my father, or for walks in the woods or over Beeston Hill with my dog.

Bob, had now been sent to Boom Defence Vessels, at first off the port of Liverpool, where he wrote to tell us of the great fires he had seen in the docks, and later off Plymouth, where he made many close friends in the dockland area. He witnessed the terrible bombing raids on the port and the destruction of vast areas of Plymouth. He had not had any leave since joining the Navy in January, but one day, 17th June, he arrived home unexpectedly, and I well remember how tearful my parents were when they saw him for the first time in naval uniform. He looked fit and well, but very tired, having come all the way from Devonport. He was in need of a wash and shave and his uniform fitted him rather badly. After a welcome cup of tea, he seemed his old self again. His leave was quite short, only six days.

In June the radio informed us that Hitler had now turned his attention towards Russia. We could hardly believe this and still thought that the Germans would invade. All sorts of rumours were going around. Badly-burnt bodies were said to have been washed ashore on the south coast. Then we heard how some German airmen had managed to row ashore from their stricken plane and had to walk to our police station to give themselves up. Some of these stories were true but we took them all with a pinch of salt.

Then word would go round the town that Princess Mary was coming to see the A.T.S. in the Grand Hotel. This proved to be true, and crowds assembled on the Leas in front of the Hotel, which was full of troops and A.T.S. The Princess arrived by car to see them march past as she stood on the steps. Next time it was the Duchess of Gloucester and we flocked to the recreation ground to see her inspect her Regiment. She received the salute, and after-wards had lunch at the Sheringham Hotel. (The Grand was de-molished in 1974. Part of the Sheringham Hotel survives as flats.)

Photo: H.H.Tansley supplied by Sheringham Museum

**Sheringham Recreation ground in use for a parade by the
Air Raid Wardens.**

Many things were difficult to obtain now. Having failed in Sheringham and Cromer, Mother and I spent an entire day going all over Norwich to get a pram for the baby. After much tiring effort we got a green and cream one for £9 10s., a lot of money in those day. The shop sent it on by rail, and a few days later it arrived safely and we stored it at my grandmother's.

Bill returned to Chatham only to be sent to Yarmouth to be interviewed for a shore job. Then he had to report to Drayton Hospital. We hardly knew what to expect, but finally he had notification that he was to leave the service in October. At the same time he heard from Yarmouth that there were prospects of a shore job.

At the end of July, I received papers from Cromer asking me to report for an interview on war work on August 11th. Of course this was expected, but when they knew I was expecting a baby, it was accepted that I could not go to any of the services or work in the munitions factories where several of my friends had gone.

67

Constantly we had news of the Cromer lifeboat being off, and of ships aground on the Haisbro sands. Nearly every day things were being washed ashore. Once, a load of oranges was scattered over the beaches. Father came home one day bringing a large wooden box still intact. Inside was lard, but covered all over with shingle, embedded in the fat. At first Mother didn't think it was any good, but they took off all the paper and melted it all down in saucepans. It was a long tiring job but they strained it all through a fine sieve into the biggest containers they could find, and it set hard. Mother said it was the best lard she had ever had and it proved to be a great standby for pastry-making. It kept perfectly well, even without a refrigerator.

At the end of October, 1941, in very rough weather, the Cromer lifeboat attempted to rescue several men from a ship, but turned over. Some of the crew were flung into the water, and the signalman, Walter Allen, was lost. He was the last of the crew to be picked up, but died shortly after. This shocked both the towns.

A miraculous episode in the service life of the *Foresters Centenary* lifeboat occurred at this time. The sea was very rough and five Polish aircrew had been drifting on a raft in the North Sea after ditching their aircraft. The landlord of the Crown Inn, Charlie Holsey, was wiping glasses near the bar and, holding one up to the light, suddenly saw this speck out at sea. This pub was the favourite of many of the lifeboat crew, and John 'Sparrow' Hardingham, the second coxswain, happened to walk in for a lunch-time drink. He was told about the raft and very quickly went off. The lifeboat was launched and, very shortly after, the five aircrew were rescued.

During that year of 1941, I became great friends with Joyce Kaye, the daughter of Frank Felmingham the local barber, who had his premises in Co-op Street. This was a wonderful meeting place for all 'shannocks' and folk who came into the town from the country for a haircut or a shave on a Saturday night. Here they would sit for hour after hour, telling all the latest yarns.

Joyce was also expecting a baby, and we often met at the clinic and in the doctor's surgery. My baby was due at the end of October and Joyce's almost at the same time, so we had much in common. Early in November my Father came home one evening saying, 'You'll have to hurry up, your chum has beaten you. She's had a little girl.'

I didn't let it bother me too much. The days came and went, and finally, after all those weeks of waiting, our son was born, weighing nine pounds, a very healthy boy. We decided to call him Christopher, as my mother said it was a lucky name. Bill was allowed home on compassionate leave for a few days.

These were the days of babies being fed every four hours; nurses and doctors said the baby should wait until the appropriate time, 6 o'clock, 10 o'clock, 2 o'clock and so on. Well we tried all this, but the baby cried and cried and cried. Mother said 'Course the child's hungry. He needs feeding; he can't wait four hours.'

My grandmother Joyful came round. This was her first great-grandchild and she took him out of his cradle and placed him on her capacious lap, saying, 'Give me a dry biscuit or a piece of bread and I'll make him some butter sop.' Mother put on the kettle or hot water and fetched some sugar, then Granny got out a small bottle of brandy and added a drop or two to the mixture, giving the baby a sip or two from the spoon. This was lapped up very quickly and the child slept for a good four hours, the first sleep we'd all had.

Bill should have gone back after three days but decided to stay an extra day. When the nurse called and walked upstairs, Bill hid in the large cupboard, but the nurse happened to spot him. 'What are you doing here?' she asked in great indignation. 'Get yourself back or I shall report you immediately.'

**Christopher in the green and cream pram –
sticky tape on the windows**

Chapter 10. Bombing and Alerts

The war dragged on. Living here on the coast we got plenty of hit-and-run raiders. Many times the alarm would go and then a few minutes later the all-clear signal. Sometimes there were so many wailings and all-clears that we wondered just what *was* happening.

When the alarm went at night, I would take my baby downstairs and Mother would get up too. We usually made a cup of tea then waited, and if the all-clear sounded we would go back to bed. The baby never cried; he seemed to take it all with good humour. Often I would lay him in his cot and then have to snatch him up and hurry downstairs again. Having no shelter, we usually dived into Mother's pantry when things were getting rather nasty. This was under the staircase, and seemed the safest place to be, as it was protected by the chimney-breast for the two downstairs rooms. It was also protected by the wall of the alleyway between the two houses, ours and Miss Mary Ann Little's next door. The Government had promised Morrison shelters to people who lived along the coastal belt, so we hoped we would be lucky enough to get one.

Early in December 1941, we awoke one morning to hear on the radio that the Japanese had bombed the American fleet in Pearl Harbour. Only a week before, the Japanese had met with the American President in a farcical pretence at peace-making. Up to this point we had been fighting alone. Now the U.S.A. came into the war not only against Japan, but also against Germany. We looked on this as a wonderful turn of events, but it was a tragic time for those people now brought into the conflict in the Far East.

It was not long after this that American troops and aircraft arrived in our country, causing much excitement. In the months that were to come, East Anglia was to be a 'Little America'. When we first saw them and heard their American drawl, we felt that they belonged to our cinema experiences. Their uniforms were so smart, and they were so friendly that I think we looked on them as film stars. When we heard rumours that Clark Gable or Jimmy Stewart was in town we would flock to the town centre to see if we could catch a sight of them. Our soldiers were immensely jealous

70

and could see themselves losing their girlfriends to these jovial lads.

January 1942 started cold and icy. We had some heavy falls of snow, and the provisions in the shops were steadily declining. We had our meagre rations and beyond that we had to improvise. It was surprising how we could make up meals from a very few items.

On January 19th we had our worst bombing so far. Mother and I had been washing all day. In those days that meant washing everything by hand, boiling, scrubbing and mangling the linen, then emptying the copper and hanging all the linen out. We had been very busy all day and the weather was bad with snow and hail, so drying the clothes was very difficult. Luckily, we had the passageway between the two houses and could hang all the large items in there. The line stretched the whole length of the house and all under cover, but it was a wretchedly cold place to hang out linen. In the freezing temperatures, you had to put on the warmest clothes, scarves, hat and coat and often gloves. We hurriedly flung them on the line and then ran indoors to get warm; but for all that it was a splendid drying area; the wind down the passage would soon blow them dry and they never got any dirt on them.

About teatime Mother and I thought we would get our meal ready. Father was working at that time on one of the aerodromes with other fishermen. The clothes (those that were dry) were brought in, and some of the baby's clothes, nappies and night-dresses, were placed up on the rack above the fireplace. We thought we would cook something hot as we knew Father would be glad of something to warm him. Then Mother decided to go to the first house at the Picture House, by the Town Clock. So we had our tea and she set off into the snow, saying to me, 'Keep your Father's dinner hot - he'll be home soon,' and away she went. The fire was blazing away and the table still laid and ready for Father.

I had just washed little Christopher, then almost two months old, and wrapped him up snugly in his cradle and he was fast asleep. The cradle was resting on the settee beside the table in the corner of the living room. The other corner held a large casement window only a few inches from the baby and me. Father came in looking cold and hungry and I set his plate before him; he was glad to be home and enjoyed his meal. He asked how we had been getting on and then looked around for the daily paper. I can see him now, enjoying his paper, the fire bright and warm, clothes airing before the fire, a scene of contentment.

71

Then, from out of the darkness, we heard a plane, extremely low; it seemed to me it was going to crash upon us. The noise of the plane was terrible and I looked at Father who turned and said, 'It's one of ours, you'll be all right.' I was trying to get to the baby and get into the pantry in my fright but his words stopped me. Then *crash!* - there was an almighty explosion, jugs, plates, cups and saucers came flying out of the pantry as if flung by a mighty hand. I shall never forget the sight of objects sailing across the room; soot came down the chimney into the fireplace in bucket-fuls, almost putting out the fire. It went in clouds across the room over the table and the food that was still on it. The soot and debris covered all the linen; we must have looked like chimney-sweeps.

I shouted to Father, 'We're hit - don't leave me!' All the lights had gone out and the window had blown right in across the table and was leaning on the baby's cradle. Christopher was screaming. Father said 'Get his bottle and give him something to drink, that'll help him.' Then he went to open the back door, which was hanging on its hinges. I tried to find the bottle and make the baby a warm milk drink. I groped about in the flickering firelight to mix sugar, baby-food and hot water, and gave it to the child, still crying, but I think if we could have actually seen what was going into that bottle we might have been rather worried. Luckily, we couldn't and the baby drank it all - he was none the worse for it.

Looking out of the broken door, we could just see, on the snow that covered the yard, large hunks of debris, bricks, mortar and huge pieces of wood. Some were balanced on the scullery roof. In the sitting room we could see that the bay window was broken, a model of my husband's ship, which he had made, was in fragments, and the front door was off its hinges.

In all the confusion we hadn't thought of Mother, but suddenly she appeared, very worried about us. News of the alarm had been flashed on to the cinema screen, and, asking someone where had been hit, she was told that it was Cremer Street. She couldn't imagine what she would find. When she got to the house she breathed a sigh of relief.

We knew that the bomb or bombs must have fallen close by, because of the dreadful noise and the state of our house. After a while, I decided to go and see what had happened. The road was covered with snow and ice and it was freezing cold. Some people had collected in the road, and soldiers and civilians were clambering over the mounds of rubble the bombs had caused, trying to look for survivors. The first victims were just four houses from us, at the corner of Salisbury Road. Mr and Mrs George Smith and their daughter Peggy had been seated at their dining table having their meal when the bomb hit; now they were all dead. Their son was away in the Army. Mr Smith had a furniture business in Church Street opposite St Peter's Church and my young cousin, Henry West, aged 18, worked for him at that time. I could see him among the group of helpers. In the road was a mobile Army canteen supplying hot food, drinks and soup for all those helping to find survivors. How they managed to do their job with everything in total darkness I do not know.

The next three houses were completely demolished. Living in them were Mrs Mary 'Rufus' West, Mr Bob Rushmer (Senior) and his wife Margaret Ann, and the next house, newly built, was owned by Eleanor Craske. It looked as if there was very little hope for these householders.

The houses across the road, although not totally demolished, were all without roofs, tiles, chimneys, and windows, a very sorry sight. Most of the people living in Cremer Street and New Road had to be evacuated from their houses, as they were almost uninhabitable. We stayed in ours that night and in the weeks to come. My close friend, Peggy Farrow, who lived in New Road was moved to a house in Morris Street.

The digging for the bodies went on all night and it wasn't until the next day that the soldiers found Mrs Margaret Rushmer. Her husband Bob had just gone to the station to meet their daughter who was expected to arrive on the London train, so fortunately he was out of the house, but what a tragedy for him and his daughter when came home to find the house completely demolished and his wife undoubtedly dead. Mrs 'Rufus' West had just gone across the road to visit her daughter-in-law, Clara, who lived in New Road, and this saved her life. As for Eleanor Craske, she was found by the rescuers after many hours of digging and taken to hospital.

We managed to go on living in our house and were thankful for our good luck in surviving. We lit candles and cleared up as much as we could. Then there was the problem of repairing the damage. Temporary measures were taken until the authorities were able to inspect the houses, and later on all the major jobs were done. We awaited the arrival of Morrison shelters with a great deal of optimism, hearing that they were very sturdy contraptions and were made with heavy steel for use indoors. I was hoping we would get one, especially now that I had a child to consider.

Soon we heard that the education authorities were to remove all the children from the elementary school at the top of Cremer Street as it was thought to be far too dangerous. The whole school was moved to several large houses further out of the town centre. These were to be temporary headquarters for the children and staff. Some went to two houses on the Rise, No.3 and No.11, and others to a house in Holway Road and also to 24 Hooks Hill Road, and another large house in Abbey Road. This was a much better arrangement for the children. Many people thought that the old site, right alongside the railway line and almost adjoining a tall tower used by the fire brigade, made it look like a small factory from the air and that German raiders would take it as such. Certainly most of the bombs we had, fell within that small area.

Father came home one day to say he was going up to the Council depot as he had heard that the Morrison Shelters were in. He went along with another fisherman and his brother Bob (Joyful), and it wasn't long before they came back carrying the sides, and pushing the top of the shelter on a barrow. It certainly was quite large and we had a problem to erect it in the sitting room. It meant pushing the two easy chairs into the corners of the room, one alongside the grandfather clock and the mahogany sideboard, the other into the bay window with the aspidistra plant in a huge jardinière. This left us only enough room to get round the Morrison shelter. The whole thing measured about 7ft by 5ft. The sides were metal but had openings so that air could circulate. The bottom had a mesh base to put a large mattress on; the four corners were made of strong steel, and the heavy steel top covered the whole thing and was held in place by nuts and bolts.

Mother soon found two large table-cloths, dark green with flowered borders, often used by fishermen's wives to make the sitting room look smart, but now to hide the hideous cage-like contraption. She even suggested putting the aspidistra on the top, but Father was very much against this.

In the years to come we were glad of this shelter. At first I still stayed upstairs to sleep, but many nights, as the raids were so frequent and bad, I decided to sleep in the shelter with my little boy. We made up a comfortable bed and sometimes Mother would

74

join me, for it was large enough to hold Christopher, Mother and me. I cannot ever remember Father sleeping in it. He would stay in bed until the last minute, and then, when the 'Jerries' got close, he would fly down the stairs, swearing and calling Hitler all the names he could think of.

I got quite used to it and felt very much safer, but later on we realized that the shelter could not protect us against a direct hit on the house. After the raid on our Street, we often saw soldiers in camouflage, crawling on all fours around the badly damaged buildings. It made an excellent area for them to exercise in.

Further tragic air-raids were to occur during the remainder of that year, 1942. We awoke one morning in July to hear that Cromer had been bombed during the early hours. Four 500lb bombs had been dropped in the centre of the town, several people had been killed and many more injured. Nine houses had been completely destroyed and quite a number so badly damaged that they had to be demolished. The main street of Cromer was a shambles. I didn't go over to see the damage, but we were sad to hear that several members of the Davies family had been killed at No 13 Garden Street, William Davies and his wife Ellen, their daughter Ann aged six, and baby son Richard John, just six months old. Ellen Davies' father and mother, Robert and Alice Bowditch were also killed. Severe damage was done to many of the town shops.

There were raids of some kind almost daily. One morning when the alarm sounded, we heard a plane flying very low and got into the shelter for safety. Some of the Ack Ack guns started firing at the raider, which proceeded to drop over 200 incendiary bombs on Beeston Common, damaging an old barn.

Then, early one morning in July, we had another dreadful raid. It was a dull, rainy day and I had been sleeping upstairs and not in the shelter. Suddenly, Mother called up the stairs, 'Get up,' she said. 'There's a Jerry hanging about. I don't like the sound of him.' We could always distinguish the sounds of German aircraft, as they had an erratic hum due to the unsynchronized engines. I picked up Christopher, now seven months old, and hurriedly went down into the sitting room and placed him straight into the shelter.

Mother was upstairs talking to my brother, who was home on leave; I heard her say 'Would you be able to see a bomb if they had just dropped one, because I think that's what he's dropped?'

I hastily clambered into the shelter. Then we heard a ship, which was off the town, firing at him. Immediately the German plane, a Dornier 217, commenced its run, swooped down with a loud whine, and discharged a cargo of bombs. By this time we had all got into the shelter - I don't know where Father was, probably looking at the sea as usual! After we heard the first explosion, we went into the living room to look out of the window and we could see a large cloud of smoke arising from the area of Beeston Road. It looked very near to Grandmother Joyful's house, just around the corner from Salisbury Road.

I hurriedly put clothes on to go and see if she was alright, and when I got to that corner a scene of devastation faced me. The four houses beyond Myrtle House (Granny's) were completely demolished and there was debris everywhere. I ran into hers, picking my way over all the bricks, mortar, and timber that lay there. Fortunately, her house wasn't joined to those that had been destroyed and she was all right.

People and rescuers were already gathering. Of the four houses that had been here, the one at the far end had Mr and Mrs Farrow living there, with my friend Peggy and her two brothers. Only the

Photo: H. H. Tansley supplied by David Craske

Beeston Road after the raid of July 27th, 1942

76

day before, I had met her pushing the pram that held her son David who had been born on March 1st. The whole family had moved to Morris Street after the raid of January 19th, but now as we chatted, she said, 'We've moved again May. We're round in Beeston Road, just moving in today. There's been a lot to do, but when we're straight you must come round.'

Now, as I stared at the wreck of the house, I could not imagine that she or any of her family was still alive. It wasn't until later in the day that we heard that Peggy and her baby and her mother had been killed. Her two young brothers had survived. Apparently, Mrs Farrow had been calling from the foot of the stairs to Peggy to get up when the bomb dropped and all three got the full impact. Peggy's husband had been home on leave but had returned that morning to his base.

It was a dreadful day. The rain was still falling as I made my way up the Avenue to see what other destruction had occurred. I knew that more bombs had fallen because of the smoke and dust. In the middle of Beeston Road, near to the Avenue, a bomb had hit a gas pipe, and there was a huge crater with flames roaring out of it. There were tiles and bricks and cement blocks all over the road; all the houses in that part of Beeston Road were very badly damaged. I made my way to Priory Road by way of Hillview Road and again came upon a scene of devastation. Priory Road certainly had taken a bashing; almost every roof was off, tiles gone, and each house severely damaged - a really terrible sight. As I walked amidst the rubble I saw an indoor air-raid shelter, perched on a crater which had once been a lovely house, now just piles of bricks and doors.

It didn't seem possible that anyone could have survived this bombing. A cousin of mine, and her husband, lived in one of these houses, but it was hard to tell which house was which. I walked further along, but was now anxious to get back home. Coming into Beeston Road, just where the Beck flows under Priory Road, I found a large Morrison shelter, crumpled and badly damaged, and nearby a woman. Inside was a little girl, the woman's daughter. I knew who they were, but I hadn't the courage to go and look at them. I knew that they were dead.

Later on that day we heard that old William Shepherd Hannah had been killed instantly with his daughter, Elsie, and granddaughter Christine, and also Mrs Martins and her two

77

daughters. The Hannah's house had received a direct hit, and their shelter, which I had seen, had been thrown a great distance. But many people, including my cousin and her husband, were saved by their indoor shelters.

There were other raids that year and much machine-gunning of fishing boats at sea. The raiders would often machine-gun the town, and one evening bombs were dropped at the top of Vincent Road, hitting a house called the Retreat, which had been used as a school. Luckily, there was no one in the house at the time.

Photo: H.H. Tansley supplied by Sheringham Museum

Vincent Road, October 1942

During the war the only person allowed to take photographs in the town was H. H. Tansley, a local photographer.

By this time I had become quite nervous. I dreaded the sirens going off. Mother had to go to my sister's in Luton as she was very ill with quinsy, and while she was away, I had to look after the cooking and the house. I was always worrying about Father at sea and also the baby. Then one day, Father came home to say if I wanted to share a house with Bob Newstead and Peggy his wife, who lived in a house right across the Common, they would be pleased for me to share it with them. This couple had taken one of 'Tooshy' Brown's children to live with them, having no children of their own. I felt it would be a good idea and, if Mother felt the same when she came home, we would go and look at the house, which was called Hebron.

78

Chapter 11. Several Moves

We heard that a number of families had moved out of the town and found accommodation with friends and relatives. Those that lived in the centre of Sheringham felt that it was wiser to move to Sheringwood or Upper Sheringham. The authorities had to find housing for those who were bombed out, as it was a very long while before houses could be rebuilt. All the damage had to be reported, forms filled in, and then the houses inspected. It wasn't until February 1943 that the houses in Cremer Street were repaired.

My grandmother had suddenly decided she would go and live for a time with her sister Polly who lived at Wickmere. Polly and her husband, Herbert, were glad to have Granny for as long as she liked. Her house in Beeston Road had not received a direct hit, but was very close to the houses which were demolished, so it was a relief to know she would be safe at Wickmere. Bill and I would cycle over to see her when he was home on leave. My parents also went over to see her, taking Christopher with them.

As soon as Mother came back from Luton, we told her about the house across the Common, and she felt we should take up the offer to share the house with Peggy and Bob. This large house, Hebron, stood quite alone across the south side of the Common, which stretched to the spring woods, away to the left of the bog area. It was painted white and had been built by Frank Pegg, and his brothers, Walter and Tom. Not far from the house was a very large oblong-shaped water pit and a large expanse of meadow with buttercups and marigolds, a very peaceful place.

We decided to go and see Peggy and Bob and have a look inside the house. It was a long walk over there from where we lived, but lovely when we got there. They said we could have the sitting room with a large bedroom and a single bedroom; this would cost us about £1 per week. Water was laid on and there was electric lighting and an indoor toilet. Bob and Peggy would have the other half of the house. The house faced due south and got all the sun through two bay windows, and there was a large garden with shrubs and fruit trees.

We didn't hesitate – we decided to take it. I had already bought some furniture and bedding of our own, so this was not a problem, but we had to arrange for all the chairs, tables, cupboards, beds, linen and crockery to be taken across the Common by horse and cart. We arranged this with Bob Newstead. He told us that coal was delivered every week and that the Co-op also delivered groceries by horse and cart. It all turned out better than we had hoped and several loads of goods made their way across the Common. There was only a cart track then and no wide paths.

I remember once going to the cinema from Hebron. Mother and Father were both at home and I left Christopher with them. When I set out across the common, making my way around the gorse bushes, it was a lovely summer evening. When I arrived at the Regent cinema, I joined a long queue. I had not thought, as I went in, that the sun would have set before I came out again. So my heart sank when I came out and realized that I had to get back across that common. The sky was darkening and I had some distance to go. Almost running, I took several short cuts between the roads (there were not so many houses as today). By the time I finally reached the Common, it was almost dark. There was just enough light to discern gorse bushes and some trees, which appeared very ghostly. I ran as hard as I could, jumping over the gorse bushes. I'm sure my feet didn't touch the ground. I must have covered the distance in record time, my imagination turning every bush into an arm out to grab me. I hurled myself up the path somehow and fell through the front door. Never again was I to go to the cinema while we lived there.

Every evening, after we had had our last meal of the day at home, Father, Mother and I, with Christopher, would go across to the house. Using the two bedrooms with a cot for the boy, we slept much better there, away from all the alarms. Father had a very long walk early in the morning before he could go off fishing with his partner. Some days I would stay up there if we heard several alarms or if it was raining. Mother usually went back home to do the cooking and shopping.

It was very pleasant living over there; we could walk out in the evening on to the Common and gather blackberries. Some evenings we stood at our bedroom windows watching Norwich being bombed. The skies were red with flames from the many buildings on fire.

One evening Bill was due home on leave from his ship. I knew what time to expect him and went to meet his train. I hadn't been able to tell him of our move, so it was going to be a surprise. As we walked off the platform, he in his naval uniform and carrying a small suitcase, we didn't turn down Station Road but began to walk across the level crossing at the end of Station Approach. He turned and said, 'What are we doing? We are going the wrong way!'

I began to realize he might not be too enthusiastic at finding we were now living a good mile away across the Common. So I replied hesitantly, 'Well after all those bombs I got a bit worried and we were up every night with the baby...there were sirens all night long, and we thought it would be a good idea to live away from the town...I hope you don't mind.' I went on to sing the praises of the house and the lovely views over the Common, and by the time we got to the white house he seemed to be reconciled. However, after two nights sleeping there and having to find our way home after he had been to have his usual at the Windham Arms or the Lobster, he began to say, 'Let's stay down at Ena Cottage. I'm fed up with all that walking.' So we did. Mother and Father still took the baby over there and we stayed at home.

The next night we had one alarm after another. I didn't get much sleep and was up most of the night. Bill was used to far more noise on board ship and he slept like a log.

At this time I was getting some problems with a swelling underneath my right jaw. I had actually had this for about seven years but had not bothered to see the doctor about it. It would swell up when I began to eat food, rather like having mumps. Mother would exclaim, 'It's because you sit in a draught near the living room window.'

For a long time it spoilt every mealtime, so eventually I went to see Dr Lawson, a friendly man whom everybody liked. As soon as he felt my jaw and neck he said, 'It's probably a blocked duct in the gland, but I'll send you to see a specialist at the Norfolk and Norwich Hospital. If you have to have an operation they will only keep you in for one day, that's all.'

The day came for me to see Mr Carruthers at the hospital at the top of St Stephens. The waiting room was full, but at last it was my turn to see the specialist. He had near him several young would-be doctors. After listening to my symptoms he turned to a nurse and said, 'Fetch her a couple of biscuits.' He directed me to a chair and told me to eat them. This I promptly did, but this time the swelling wasn't very pronounced.

'It comes up much larger when I am eating a meal.'

Giving me a strange look he said, 'Do you think you're going to have a meal on the hospital?' Taken aback, I just stared at him. He then turned to the students and said to them, 'What is your opinion of this?' They all made replies similar to one another; one said a *ranula*, another a *saliva calculus* and so on. Finally, turning to me, he said, 'This is probably a *saliva calculus* and you will need to come into hospital to have an operation.'

He must have thought I was a complete idiot when I naively said, 'Could I come in when my husband is on leave?' He gave me a withering look and said something to the effect that fitting in with the Royal Navy was out of the question. This was on May 28th, and it was some time before I had my operation.

Bill had been aboard a number of escort vessels and sloops, but on May 18th he left Chatham Barracks to join H.M.S. *Woodcock* at Glasgow, these warships were all named after birds, *Snipe, Starling, Wild Goose, Kite*, and others. These vessels were to become famous as the 'Killer' group under Captain F. J. Walker, the most successful U-Boat hunter of all in the Battle of the Atlantic. They were constantly coming in to Liverpool and reporting several enemy submarines sunk.

Bill never said much about his activities on this ship but I knew he was happy aboard a small vessel. Later he was to tell me about their vast searches in areas trying to get the enemy below. They would listen for submarines using Asdic to get positions, then drop depth charges. Sometimes oil and clothes, and other debris, would come to the surface, but they knew this could be a ploy by the enemy to make them believe the U-Boat had been sunk and get the ship to leave the spot. So the cat-and-mouse game continued until the naval commander on board was satisfied they had been successful.

Bill arrived home for his first leave from *Woodcock* on June 26th. He told us how each ship searched a patch of several square miles for U-Boats, and would sit over one for hours making sure it was sunk. As top cover they had R.A.F. Flying Boats, which could spot the U-Boats in advance from the air.

He brought us chocolate bars from Newfoundland. What

luxury! On Russian convoys up in the Arctic Circle, his ship had got covered with ice and had to come into harbour in Scotland to be de-iced. He certainly seemed happier on the *Woodcock*, and

H.M.S. Woodcock

much enjoyed the comradeship. His next leave came for a few days in August. This time he didn't look forward to going back, but accepted it as necessary.

Sometimes my brother Bob would also get home on leave from Plymouth. He was very glad when some of his mates, like 'Tooshy' Brown, were on leave too, but he dreaded going back. We noticed how quiet he was on his last day and he was adamant that no one was to go to the station to see him off, but each time, as he went out, I would put my hat and coat on and make my way discreetly to the station by another route. I would hide in a building near the level-crossing gates and wait until his train drew out of the station. In this way I would get a last glimpse of him. These were some of the worst times during the war, when they had to leave; we would go sadly home, never knowing if we would see them again.

At this point Bob Newstead told us that he and his wife were moving to a little house on the Cromer Road and, if we liked, we could take over Hebron ourselves. Well, this was quite unexpected

83

and I thought perhaps we would have to move back home. Then one day a Mrs Crowe called at Mother's house and said she had heard about Hebron and wondered if we would share the house with her and Mr Crowe. It seemed a perfect solution, as she also wanted to be away from the town. We explained that it was quite a long walk over there but that we enjoyed it, and we left her to think about it. A few days later they decided to move, and on December 9th they had their furniture moved over the Common.

Doctor Lawson hadn't heard anything from Norwich Hospital about my operation so I decided to write to them. Within a couple of days, a letter came to say they wanted me to see Dr Burfield, the surgeon who was to operate, on Tuesday Ocobert 12th. Again, I went by train to see him and, as a result, I was told to be at the Hospital on Ocobert 25th for the operation.

When that day arrived, Mum and Dad went with me by train and we walked to the hospital in St Stephens. I was soon put in the Burton-Fanning ward. The following day I was prepared for the operation and ready to have it done, but the doctor came to see me about 11.30 a.m. saying I would have to wait until the following Tuesday. I was very upset about this as I had been prepared, and had no food, so I blurted out, 'Oh please get it done today, I don't want to wait that long.'

Surprisingly, he said 'I will just go to the theatre and see if there is any chance of it being done today.' Within a few minutes, two orderlies came with the trolley and I was wheeled hurriedly to the operating theatre.

Later that afternoon I came round, feeling pretty awful and wondering where I was. My poor mouth and jaw were very sore, and for many days I was hardly able to eat or drink. It wasn't until the food they brought me kept being returned that anyone realized that my swallowing was so bad. Then Dr Burfield very kindly came to see me and inspected my mouth. He said the tongue was lopsided but would eventually right itself. The sub-lingual gland had had to be removed as it was full of stones and, if not removed, would get worse; it was also fibrous but would heal in time.

I had great difficulty chewing, so was kept mainly to liquids. There were about 36 beds in the ward I was in, so the nurses had a great deal to do. As it was autumn, the light faded quite early in the day and all the windows had to be blacked out. Only the week before I went in, the ward above me had received a hit, and from the veranda we could see burnt mattresses and pillows lying on the grass outside. My bed was put out on the veranda with others in the morning, but the orderlies would have to start blacking out all the windows at about 2.30. Then we were all wheeled into the main ward, which was so cramped for space that the beds from outside would be put head to tail, completely filling the ward. The nurses must have had a job to get to the patients.

If there were raids, they said we would not be aware of it until the enemy planes were overhead. I don't think we were too worried, but one night the alarm went and some of the very ill patients, who couldn't get out of bed, were very frightened. Those that could, were told they could get under their beds. From where I lay, I could look along the corridor, full of beds, and see the doctors, nurses and orderlies all wearing their tin helmets. Soon patients were trying to get underneath their beds. It was comical to see people grabbing their handbags as if their lives depended on them, or making their faces up before diving beneath the beds. I just lay there, thinking that I might as well stay in bed as crawl under it. Then the all-clear sounded and peace was restored.

My sister Ena came all the way from Luton to see me, which I thought was most kind of her, as it was not an easy journey. Mum and Dad came quite often, but if I tried to talk to them it put my temperature up. Dr Burfield came and saw me, and said that the wound had turned septic and had to be drained, so for a few days I must have no visitors. He was most kind at all times and came and sat on the end of my bed one day to reassure me that the throat and mouth would heal eventually. He laughed and said to me, 'When you go out of here, we are going to put a notice on you to say 'unique', as this operation you have had is quite rare.'

I was there for fourteen days. So much for Dr Lawson saying I would only be in for a day!

When I came home, the first thing to greet me was the news that Mr and Mrs Crowe didn't want to stay at Hebron; they found it very inconvenient. This gave me a problem because I couldn't rent the house by myself. We stayed until the end of December 1942, and little Chris took his first steps at Hebron. We now had the problem of moving all our possessions back home, but another close friend, Kathy Gant, who lived in Brook Road with her husband Charlie Sadler, who was in the Army, very kindly offered part of her house and we moved there on January 1st 1943.

Hebron was a fine building, but was demolished some years ago to make way for a housing estate. We had some happy days there. Many times we hurriedly collected all the things I needed, such as dried milk for the baby, nappies, clothes and food and put them all in the pram to get away from the threat of being bombed, especially on rainy days.

Once my brother came all the way over there bringing things I needed. 'If your name's on a bomb, you'll get it wherever you are,' he would say moodily, and, strange to say, after the war ended we heard that a German bomb had been found in the bog nearby.

Chapter 12. Brightening Skies

We now settled in at Kathy's. It was nice of her to share her home; we had been friends for many years and, with Charlie away like Bill, it made company for us both. We still had beautiful views across the Furrow Common and a newt pond to visit with Christopher. It was lovely and peaceful, to see the sunrise over Beeston Priory each morning, a far cry from the horrors of war.

We got on well together, sharing the chores, shopping and cleaning, and Dad would often walk up of an evening so that we could get out to the cinema. Not long after we moved in, Bill came home unexpectedly and was told we had moved to Brook Road. He was quite happy to hear this, as it was a bit more civilized.

Bill told us he was probably going abroad as all the ship's company had been given foreign service leave of seven days. He was worried about his kitbag, which he had accidentally left on the train. There were bags of sugar in it to help us out, and he wondered if he would get a stiff reprimand if found out. We had to find a telephone box to contact the lost parcels office to find out where the kitbag was. Luckily for Bill, it was found at Melton Constable station and a Sheringham porter at our station kindly got it and brought it to us, with the sugar still intact.

The next day we made a visit to Lowestoft, taking little Chris to see all Bill's relations before going abroad. We had a lovely day out and got home by 7 p.m. Bill wasn't too happy to be going abroad but said it had to be, as the war in the Far East had become very intense.

In Brook Road, a few doors from Kathy, lived Mary Dennis. She would often come in to see us and have a chat. Her husband John, known to everybody by his family nickname of 'Jodrell', was in the R.A.F. and she was glad of the company now and again. Her daughter and two sons were quite young and, like every wife in wartime, she was anxious for her husband's safety. They were a nice family. One day she came to tell us that she had just heard that his plane had been shot down over Hanover and the crew were missing. We were very worried for her, but she took the news bravely.

Not many days later, she came again to say that she had heard Lord Haw Haw in one of his usual broadcasts, giving out the names of airmen and soldiers who had baled out or been captured. To her amazement, he mentioned John's name and said he was safe and well in a German hospital, being looked after with other members of his crew. She was crying with joy when she told us - it was such a relief. John was later to return home, largely recovered after his ordeal, although lame.

In May, 1943, we decided to go back to Cremer Street to live. Christopher was now running everywhere, and loved to be with his granddad. Sleeping once more in the air-raid shelter, he and I got a fairly good night's rest. Raids over England by German bombers were still intense. The night they raided Coventry, Bob was on leave, and we listened to the constant drone of aircraft overhead; it seemed to go on for ages, never ceasing. We realized that it must be a big raid somewhere; the sound of aircraft went on for a long time, then gradually subsided. Bob said, 'I don't like the sound of that, do you? Somebody is getting it bad tonight.'

All was quiet for about a couple of hours, and then we heard the raiders returning home. Next day we knew that Coventry had taken the brunt of the Luftwaffe raid.

Daily we saw our British and Allied bombers going out to raid Germany and the occupied countries. By night, wave after wave would come from the west, probably Lincolnshire, heading north east or easterly, for Berlin, the Rhur, and Hamburg. During daylight hours, we would watch the American planes assemble overhead in preparation for their raids. Above us, on those lovely summer mornings, were layer upon layer of heavy bombers, B24 Liberators and B17 Flying Fortresses, circling and circling again. It was awe-inspiring to see them, loaded with bombs, ready to head off for whatever fate held for them. We could only watch and pray.

After they had collected, they flew off, and silence prevailed. Later we would hear the drone of aircraft returning, and we would go out to watch those who were fortunate enough to make it back to England, sometimes coming in quite low, limping home badly damaged. We could see great gaping holes and torn fuselage; some would be flying on three propellers and some on two. Many times we saw only one engine working, the pilot coming in on a wing and prayer, flying lopsided, and we marvelled at the skill of the pilot in getting the aircraft home.

Some nights the raids by the Germans would be bad, and the searchlights and the 'crump' of bombs kept us awake. Often, when our planes returned at night, German planes would mix in with them, and it would be difficult for the Ack Ack gunners on the ground to pick out the enemy. The enemy planes would then drop hundreds of incendiaries.

During that lovely summer, we would often go down to the beach. There were very few visitors these days, so the townsfolk had the beaches all to themselves. Barbed wire entanglements were all along the promenade and the stones, but there were some places that allowed access. Military personnel were everywhere and we had to ask to be allowed through. (The ban on entry to beaches was not lifted until August 25, 1944)

As well as the barbed wire, there were large concrete blocks built as tank traps, some in Beach Road and some on the area of the tank shelter. Once I was on the East Promenade with my son, then about eight months old, when along came a Jerry plane flying very low from the east and firing its machine guns. The people standing there, watching the fishermen, all ran to the pill-box on the tank shelter, and tried to squeeze into its small entrance. Some fat fellow got almost wedged in the doorway with the rest of us still outside and eager to get in. The first thought in my mind was to get my son in if I could, so I pushed like the rest. We all got inside at last, but by this time the plane had gone.

Bus transport during the war must have been quite good, for my diary for August 1943 says that we all went to see Grandmother Joyful at Wickmere near Aldborough, where she was living with Aunt Polly and her family. Mother, Father and I took Christopher, Aunt Bessy and Aunt Myrtle, both Wests, to see her. The small cottage, had a well just outside the kitchen door. It was covered with a heavy wooden lid, but I hardly dare let Christopher out of my sight for fear of him falling in. Grandmother was reasonably happy there and anyway she couldn't go home until her house was restored after the bombing of 1942. By the October of 1943 she had returned home to Beeston Road.

On 9th August we heard the sad news of Douglas Slade being lost over Hamburg; he was a nice young man in the R.A.F., who had visited us several times whilst based in Lincolnshire. He was brother-in-law to my sister. A few weeks later, I read in the *Cromer Post*, of the loss of Bert Woodrow on September 3rd. He too was in the R.A.F. on bombing missions; I knew this would devastate his family who lived in Holt. I had known and liked Bert very much, and had been out with him before I met Bill. Constantly we were hearing of the loss of someone we knew and it was hard to take, but everyday life had to go on.

We still listened to Winston Churchill, when he spoke on the radio. He was always eloquent and could make a great speech that spurred us on. The war situation was brighter now and we were being given better news. In September of that year, 1943, the 8th Army had invaded Italy; there had been very little resistance, and on the 8th September an armistice was signed with Italy.

At home, there was always the brighter side. We young wives, who had our husbands away in the forces, appreciated the advantages of living at home with our parents, who shared the chores and the rent and helped to look after our children. Young Christopher wanted to go everywhere with his Granddad; Father could hardly get rid of him. He would get him on his knee and tell him stories from the Bible, but he managed to introduce Sheringham characters into them. The Ark, I remember, was stranded on Sheringham Beach. There were also stories about how the tar barrel got alight, and how the lifeboat was launched, which had to be repeated time and time again. He would even go with

**Four generations: May with her father and
Grandmother Joyful with Christopher**

90

Father when he went to the Windham Arms; Bob Olley, the landlord, didn't seem to mind. He sometimes dropped dominoes in the glasses of beer, but no one complained.

My sister bought Christopher a little second-hand tricycle, which he would ride up and down the pavement outside our house. There wasn't the traffic to worry about in those days. One day, he left it around the corner of Hastings Lane (off Cremer St) and Mr Charlie Dennis ('Jo Willie' the butcher), came along in his van and ran over the little trike. It was a complete wreck, and poor Christopher was very upset. Mr Dennis gave him something, but unfortunately it didn't make up for losing the trike.

Another day, Mother came home from Old Nelson's up the road with a jar of honey from under the counter. She placed the jar on the table with other items, and had just turned away, when there was a sudden crash as the jar of honey hit the hearth tiles. We couldn't believe our eyes. The unexpected treat was no more; it lay in a splodge of honey mixed with broken glass on the hearth. Little Chris seemed as surprised as we were. We couldn't scold him; he had no idea how precious the item was and how difficult to obtain.

For Christmas or birthdays, we would try all sorts of things to pretty things up, like making chocolate icing from cocoa and treacle - if we could get the treacle. To trim the Christmas tree we collected tin foil to make into stars or fairies for the tree. If we had sweets with pretty wrappers, they were all saved - there was precious little we threw away.

After clothing coupons came into force in 1942, we had mostly to wear the same old clothes. It was very difficult to obtain material for dressmaking or wool for knitting. The whole country's effort was geared to the production of armaments and aircraft.

Christopher was very prone to attacks of bronchitis and asthma during the winter months. We were under a Dr G. at the time and one Saturday the little boy seemed quite ill and in need of the doctor. I went to his house in Augusta Street, and he came and gave me a tablet for the child. Later that afternoon, my father, who had been sitting beside his cot, decided to lift him out on to his lap for a while. Mother and I were having a welcome cup of tea in the other room, when suddenly Father called, 'Mother, come quick!'

She saw immediately that Christopher was seriously ill and, taking him in her arms, she tried to revive him. Panic-stricken, I ran for the doctor, but when I got to his house, I was told he was away for the rest of the day. Father, who had followed me, decided to fetch Dr Lawson, who lived in St Nicholas Place, saying at the same time, 'I think it's too late. I think the little boy has gone.'

Doctor Lawson was aware it was another doctor's case, but after listening to my father, he hurriedly fetched his car and rushed off to our house in Cremer Street. It was night-time now and very dark. There were queues of people waiting at the cinema near the Town Clock. I remember running past, terrified to think what I should find when I got back to the house. In fact I didn't want to go back, and I sat on the low wall near the Salvation Army Hall, crying. Suddenly Dr Lawson appeared and put his arm around my shoulders saying, 'Come back home, and you will see your little boy is perfectly all right, but I want you to fetch Nurse Howlett from Holway Road as soon as possible.'

Nurse Howlett was soon on her way. Christopher had had convulsions, and Mother had done the right thing at the crucial moment. With the help of the doctor and the nurse, he recovered. We sat up all night with him and, strangely enough, the next day Christopher was full of beans.

Brother Bob and Christopher

Chapter 13. Sadness and Loss

January 1944 opened as usual with very cold and frosty weather. It had been a dreary winter, but now we looked forward to more peaceful times. Before that could be, the invasion of Europe and the defeat of the Nazis must take place.

At the same time, we were being warned over the radio and in the newspapers of Hitler's secret weapons. We thought this might be bluff, but it wasn't safe to under-estimate the might of the German Army. By this time, however, Germany was itself was being subjected to R.A.F. bombing raids at night and the U. S. Air Force raids during daylight. It was one of these daylight raids by the U. S. Air Force, on January 4th, that gave my father the shock of his life.

When the weather was too bad for him to go to sea, he loved to take one of his jaunts into the woods. He had made himself a small barrow to collect wood for the fire, and usually he would take Christopher with him, all wrapped up warm in his siren suit. He much preferred to go along Holway Road and up to Pretty Corner. The land on the right-hand side of the road there was all owned by Mr Upcher, who lived at Sheringham Hall, and woe betide any one caught by his gamekeeepers, so my father had enquired whether it was all right to collect any branches that had blown down. The Squire, who knew my father, was quite willing to agree to this.

Father never sawed anything down, but collected odd bits and pieces and put them in sacks on the barrow to push home, usually with Christopher riding on top. This day, however, was very cold, with flurries of snow, and Father said, 'Tha's too cold today to take the boy. It wouldn't be fit in this weather.'

He set off about 2.30, and whilst he was in the field near Butts Lane he heard the intermittent sound of aircraft engines in trouble. Looking up, he could see the aircraft, which appeared to be trying to land in the field. He knew by the sound of it that it was going to crash and didn't know whether to run out into the field or take cover in the woods nearby. Later he told us how frightened he was and said, 'I'm suffin glad I didn't hev that boy with me. Whatever should I hev dun?' He had just decided to run into the woods, when the plane, a B24 Liberator, tore into the trees. The noise was terrible; branches were flying everywhere as the great plane broke up, and then there was silence. He expected it to explode, and then he heard cries of help from the men inside the wrecked plane and went back.

The wreckage was in the corner of the field and the plane had caught the tops of the trees in trying to make an emergency landing. The main cockpit area had ploughed into an earth bank. One of the men had either been flung out, or had managed to get out of the wreck. Father told us how he got up into the wreck to try to help the crew, but he knew by the look of some that they were dead. Other people were rushing from the fields nearby to help. Father gave some of the wounded airmen cigarettes and then sent some boys to phone for an ambulance.

The Liberator, from its base at Wendling near Dereham, had been on a raid to Kiel Canal that day with a crew of ten. Four of the crew were killed and others badly injured. When Father came home to tell us all about it, his clothes stank of petrol. He was very upset and often wondered if the other men survived the crash. Later that day, when Mother and I walked up to the crash site, many American personnel were there, and a huge crane was trying to lift out the wreckage. As we stood and watched, it seemed amazing that anyone could have survived the crash and lived to tell the tale.

Fifty years later, with the generous help of Doug and Celia Willis, we were able to erect a memorial stone at Upper Sheringham Church as a tribute to all the crew of that plane and to hold a service in their memory. Over twenty near relatives came from the U.S.A. to be with us all, and we were honoured to have there the only surviving crew member, Mr Henry Wilk, his wife, son and daughter-in-law, and Doris Reiche the widow of the young pilot.

We were now hearing reports that the Russian Army was making headway against the Germans and had advanced over fifteen miles into Poland. This was good news and soon we were looking forward to hearing that our troops had landed in France. According to the papers, General Montgomery was coming back to England to begin planning the second front. Most days we would see lorry loads of troops in the town and everywhere the military were training. Cremer Street still had some derelict buildings that

94

were ideal places to practice their manoeuvres. They would creep along on all fours, covered with camouflage, faces blackened, often down the alleyway dividing our house from the next-door neighbour's.

One day in April, I took my little son in his pushchair up through the Springs Woods, and as we were returning past the Common, a large contingent of cars was coming up the lane, it consisted of several large automobiles flying Union Jacks and being escorted by military outriders. I knew it must be someone very important, maybe the King. As they came nearer to us, the outriders came forward to open the large gate to that part of the lane to allow the convoy through. I glanced into the large car as it drove slowly past me, and recognized General Montgomery.

I thought it was worth going back up the lane to get a further look. I was suddenly aware that the cars had stopped and the passengers were alighting to go across the Common to inspect the troops on manoeuvres. Standing on one side was a sergeant with his arm raised to stop anyone else passing. I asked him if I could go further but got a stern refusal. He did just admit that it was General Montgomery.

I could see all the important personnel making their way across the rough ground and when they arrived at a large pill box that had been built there, Monty got up to speak to the troops and give them encouragement. Seeing this, although it was all 'hush-hush', I felt sure that the invasion of France was getting nearer.

At Easter my sister came home for a few days with her husband, Don; it was a happy weekend for us all as she gave us the surprising news that she was expecting her first baby in October. They had been married for eight years and she had always made a great fuss of Christopher. So we began buying wool to knit for the happy event.

Hitler's rockets, fired from Europe, were now finding their targets on our side of the Channel; places on the south and southeast coast were getting badly hit by these deadly weapons. They sounded awesome, but we were told these were Hitler's last efforts, so people had to grin and bear it. When the 'doodle-bugs' came over our part of Norfolk we had several alarms, but fortunately Sheringham had nothing worse than one near miss. We heard of one landing near Matlaske and one in the countryside nearby, but these were never confirmed.

During the war years there was a small oasis where we could take our children, almost in the centre of the town and easily reached. Many of us young mums would collect there with our children and they could run around in the grass taking no harm. It was kept in good condition by the Council and had seats and flower beds. Today this is the putting green near the station, but in those days it was warm and sheltered from the cold sea breezes.

Like other young women, my Sister Ena had been 'called up', and had been working at the Vauxhall Motor Works, where Don also worked. It was only about a mile from their home. She now wrote home to say that she was suffering from swollen ankles and hands and seeing flashing lights before her eyes. Mother advised her to leave the job as she felt it was doing her no good, but my sister continued with the work for some time, as she felt it her duty to stay as long as she could. She was constantly making produce for her store cupboard and was an excellent manager, very independent and honest. We were busy making things for the coming baby and hunting everywhere for the required articles, which were getting harder to find.

Just before the invasion of Europe by the Allies, Bill came home on leave. As usual, we enjoyed those few days together with others also on leave; he went fishing with my father at every opportunity and also took Christopher out. When Bill went back to Portsmouth, he said some words, as we waited at Sheringham station, that made me think the invasion was imminent. 'Now I don't want you to worry about me if you don't hear anything for a while. You know what's on. I can't say anything, but please don't worry.' Then he kissed me, got into the train and waved goodbye. I little knew then that I should indeed have cause to worry.

Large lorry-loads of troops were everywhere and the soldiers we knew hinted that they were 'on their way'. Hundreds of people lined the main streets to see convoy after convoy move off: tanks, guns, artillery, N.A.A.F.I., jeeps, armoured vehicles. It was a thrilling sight. Our hearts were with those men as they prepared for the beachheads wherever they might to be.

On June 6th we awoke to the news that the invasion had started at dawn on the coast of Normandy. All that day we saw further lorries going, and the radio informed us that a big naval force of 4000 ships was off France. We sat by our radios all day listening to speeches made by the King, Churchill, Montgomery, and Eisenhower. We had great hopes of victory, but our most earnest prayers were for the welfare of all those men in conflict over there.

On 13th June, Bill came home unexpectedly, late at night, looking extremely tired. His ship had been in collision during the D-Day landings and was in port for repairs, so he had been granted leave. Whilst home, he went to sea again with my father, whose partner at that time had lost his wife very suddenly. When his leave ended, Father gave him some cooked lobsters to take back for his first lieutenant. Well a couple of weeks went by and all I got from Bill were letters very much out of date. This was quite usual and nothing to worry about, but one evening, I had been for a walk to look at the sea, and as I strolled home, I was very surprised to see a policeman on our front doorstep. I went down the passageway between the two houses and there I found another policeman, tapping on the back door. This certainly took me by surprise and, wondering what could warrant a visit from the police, I asked them what was wrong? They said, 'We've come to search the house as your husband is a deserter.'

I was absolutely astounded, and Mum and Dad were as distressed as I was. I immediately said, 'My husband would never be a deserter, whatever are you talking about?' They still insisted on searching the house but stopped when my father got very upset and said, 'You can search all you like, my son-in-law is not here. He went back to his ship on Saturday night. I gave him a couple of lobsters to take back with him.'

They then angered me further by saying, 'Has he got another woman anywhere?'

I was most indignant and said, 'Of course not! He must be hurt somewhere or even killed.' There had been a bad raid on London on the night he went back and it was the first thing that entered my head. I was of course very worried as well as upset, knowing full well that Bill was not the sort of man to miss his ship, without good cause. Eventually the policemen left and we could only wait for news.

The next day I went to the police station and there on the wall was a notice about three sailors deserting their ships. Bill's name was up there, but there seemed to be nothing we could do. I sent a wire to my father-in-law who was duly alarmed, but we had to be patient and await further news from Bill. A week went by and I heard nothing, but this was not unusual as when the ships were at sea I might often go twenty-one days before getting a letter. I tried very hard not to worry; knowing Bill, there was no likelihood of him being a deserter. Then Mother came up with an idea.

'Why don't you go and see Colonel Atkinson? I believe he might possibly find out what has happened.' Colonel Atkinson was a member of the S.S.A.F.A. (Soldiers, Sailors and Air Force Association), who lived in a large house called Hilbre in Holway Road. I went there straight away and he was very kind and helpful, saying that he would look into it immediately, He asked me if it was possible that Bill would desert, and I said, 'No, never.'

I had to wait another ten days, but then I got a message from Colonel Atkinson, saying that my husband was quite safe and well, but in the confusion he had to join another ship as it left Portsmouth. He wasn't aware that his ship had reported him as a deserter. So all was well that ended well. We often laughed about it in later years because one of the policemen who came that day became a near neighbour.

Besides writing to my husband and brother, I wrote regularly to Eric Wink in the Navy, somewhere in the Middle East, to Cliff Lakey in the R.A.F. proceeding through Italy, and to Jimmy Bishop, whom we called 'Chibbles,' who was in Ceylon. When he first had his draft papers, he had said jokingly, 'I'm sure to go somewhere nice and hot. I can see myself lying under a palm tree and eating coconuts. We all laughed at this but it came to be just about true.

My friend Joyce and I kept up a correspondence with two or three soldiers we had got to know, who were now across the Channel winning back parts of occupied Europe. The letters continued up until the crossing of the Rhine and then stopped. We never knew if they survived.

Early in the month of August, my sister left her job. She was under the care of a gynaecologist, and would go to a good nursing home to have her baby. But on the Monday, 21st August, Mother received a telegram from Don, asking her to go to Luton as Ena was very ill and had been taken to the nursing home. I helped Mother get things together for her journey, then, having no telephone, I went to an uncle, whose shop had a phone, and he kindly allowed me to phone Don. He gave me a very alarming picture of my sister's symptoms.

Sister Ena, aged 25

The following day I had to see Dr Lawson to explain why my Mother couldn't keep an X-ray appointment. When I told him Ena's symptoms and the stage of her pregnancy, he threw up his hands and said something I couldn't understand, but I knew by his face how serious it was.

The next few days were very trying. We could get no actual news of her progress from the nursing home. I phoned daily but was only told that she was very ill, unconscious in fact, and that they were going to take the baby away from her. Mother wrote to us, but she was never allowed to see Ena, which was very upsetting for her. We felt helpless at home; we could only pray. At night we got very little sleep because of the aircraft overhead, the searchlights criss-crossing the sky and the noise of distant bombs.

On the Saturday, when I phoned, I was told Ena had been moved to the Luton and Dunstable Hospital and had been given three blood transfusions. On the Sunday we were told she was very ill, and Don later phoned to say a baby girl (still-born) had been delivered at 1 o'clock. Dolly Pegg, a relation of Mr West whose phone we had been using, had come along to give us the news. I remember saying to her, 'Now Dolly, let's hope she will begin to improve.' Sadly that was not to be.

On the following Tuesday night Mr West came to bring us the sad news of her death from eclampsia and also to tell my Father to go on the train to Luton the next day. However, while we were getting his clothes ready, Mr West came again to say that she was to be brought home for burial, as this had been her last wish.

This was a really sad time for us all; it hit my mother and father very hard indeed. She was only 36 years old. I sent news to my brother, and he was able to come home for her funeral, but Bill couldn't get leave.

Hitler was now bent on sending over the V2 rockets. These appalling weapons of destruction could destroy whole streets of houses and devastate a large area. Our forces were now making remarkable progress in Europe, however, and the Russian Army was advancing on Berlin. It was only a matter of time before these huge armies met and we would eventually be at peace.

Chapter 14. A Brighter Dawn

The news from the Far East war zone was very bad. Day after day we heard depressing news. Things were going especially badly for those who had been sent out to Singapore. The Royal Norfolks, who had been stationed here along with the Cambridgeshire Regiment, had left these shores for the Far East. When we heard of the fall of Singapore to the Japanese forces our hearts sank.

In November 1944, when Bill came home on leave, he was certain that H.M.S. *Woodcock* would soon be on her way out there, and we knew that, if he went, it would mean a long parting. His ten-day leave had been extended, making it nearly three weeks. Bob had also had leave at the same time, and it was lovely for them to be together. I saw him go away on 20th November, and the *Woodcock* sailed for the Far East at the end of that year. We were not to see each other again until 1946, after the end of the war with Japan

The Allies' advance across Europe was gaining momentum, and we seemed to be sleeping more easily in our beds. I still preferred to sleep in the indoor shelter with Christopher. Almost everything was still in short supply, bread, flour, sugar, tea, even the bare necessities.

Christopher liked having a train ride to see the huge American bombers on the way to Norwich. At Rackheath, which was close to Salhouse station, the large airfield stretched right down to the railway line, and as we drew into the station we could see the bombers parked very close, many painted with emblems and names, such as Saucy Sue and Lilli Marlene. Many had brightly-coloured tails. Chris never wanted to go into Norwich, so we used to come back on the next train.

For the many people who had husbands, sons or brothers captured by the Japanese, it was very hard, for they got no news of their loved ones. An aunt of mine, May Fields, had three sons, all in different war zones; her eldest, Ashleigh, was captured by the Japanese and spent a long while in Changi jail, and on the Burma Railway. She heard no news of him at all, and the weeks and months extended into years with still no news. She took it all very bravely. Then one day, I was in her little cottage when a card was delivered. She couldn't make head or tail of it. 'What is it?' she said, 'Has he been killed?'

The card was plain, no date or postmark, only a very few hand-written words, 'I am well' in a very tiny space at the bottom, and then his name, 'Ashleigh'. I said to her 'He's all right my dear, Ashleigh is alive and well.' But of course several long months had gone by since that card had been sent and there was no certainty that he was still alive.

Later, he was to return with all the other prisoners of war, looking gaunt and frail, almost like a walking skeleton. It took him many years to become fit enough to work; in fact he never fully recovered from his ordeal. Aunt May's youngest son, Tom, was killed in Italy.

News from my husband was very scarce; his letters were ever more heavily censored. There were more holes cut in them than words, so we couldn't guess at his whereabouts. Later, after the war, when he finally arrived home, we heard that his ship had been attached to the American Fleet and had taken part in many of the battles for the islands of Malaysia. He had also enjoyed the warm hospitality of the Australian people. After several weeks of conflict, the ship's company would be given shore leave. Half of them would stay with Australian families for two or three weeks and then the other half would go. One Christmas, he stayed with a family in Sydney and had Christmas pudding on Bondi Beach. Another time, they went to Brisbane and stayed on a ranch with a very kind family called Weston. He had a great time there and was offered a job and a house out there, if we wanted to go, but we chose to stay in Norfolk.

Bill spoke very highly of the American servicemen. 'When they take over an island,' he said, 'they first make a good runway for aircraft, but the next thing they do, would you believe it, is to land large casks of ice-cream and all the essentials to keep the personnel happy.' He brought home photos of him and his mates on Manus Island. He was told there was a nurse from Sheringham there, but he never got to meet her.

Gradually things were improving here in England as the German Army retreated before the combined might of the Allies. It was a race to see whether the Americans and British or the Russians would get to Berlin first. There were not so many air-raids now and we slept a bit more peacefully. Then came the wonderful news that our forces were celebrating victory over the Nazis. Berlin had fallen, Adolf Hitler and his mistress were dead, and many of his high-ranking officers and generals had been captured.

At last, Winston Churchill, in another of his magnificent speeches, proclaimed the great news of V.E. Day. Lights would go on again all over the world.

Celebrations were to take place in towns and villages, and my friend Joyce and I went everywhere trying to buy red, white and blue ribbon. Father suddenly produced a very large white ensign. I don't know where he got it from or where it went after to afterwards, but Father hung it from the front bedroom window, fastening its pole to the bedstead. It was so big that it was touching the roof of the bay window below.

Other flags soon appeared. What a glorious occasion it was, and with what joy and pride were the decorations finally found and put out! The shops had not been supplied with suitable goods and it was very hard even to get ribbons, but, after much searching, we found coloured ribbons to tie in our hair, and put out anything that was red, white and blue.

That evening there was dancing in the streets with accordions and pianos for music. Then, when the lights came on, great cheers went up. No more blackouts, no more groping in the dark. What added to our genuine happiness was the knowledge that those who had survived would eventually return home. I was glad for my friends, whose husbands were somewhere in Europe, but a little sad to know that we had to win victory over Japan before Bill would be able to get home.

May 8th 1945 was V.E. Day, when the war with Germany was officially over. There was great rejoicing everywhere, relayed to us over the radio and in the cinema newsreels, but I had to live with the possibility of the war with Japan lasting perhaps another two years. There had been so many setbacks out there, so many islands captured by the Japs; even Australia was threatened with invasion. The outlook was grim, but we had confidence in the might of the American forces.

Some good news came in March when Iwo Jima was captured after 72 days of intensive fighting. Then the Phillippines, lost in 1942, were re-taken by General McArthur. The next wonderful news came in June when we heard that a great battle, which had lasted for 80 days, had resulted in the capture of Okinawa. We also learned that the Japanese had suffered great losses of men, captured or killed. We had hope at last.

Strangely, the dropping of the atomic bombs on Hiroshima and Nagasaki did not get great headlines. We don't seem to have been given the news on the day after the bombs were dropped. I was casually looking at the *Daily Mail* when a very small paragraph caught my eye and, as I read it, I felt that something extraordinary had taken place. I said to my Mother, 'I don't know what sort of bombs they have dropped in Japan, but there are thousands of people killed and great devastation.' We didn't comprehend the significance of those bombs, but we would soon know the outcome.

About this time, my friend Margaret, who lived in Devon, came up to visit us. She had many old friends in the area and it made a lovely break. We thought we would go to Norwich; now that the war was over, it could be a peaceful jaunt. We looked in some of the shops, then, as we walked along Gentlemen's Walk, decided to go into Backs, a well-known inn in the City. The whole place was packed with Americans; there was no place to sit and hardly anywhere to stand. The atmosphere was extremely jovial and jolly. The City of Norwich was well-liked by the American forces; it provided all those men and boys, so far from home, with welcome relief from their hazardous job. There were so many bases in the villages surrounding Norwich and the whole of East Anglia that it was called 'Little America'. Whenever we went to Norwich we would see these young men in their smart uniforms, standing outt amongst our drabness. The Americans felt grateful for the way Norfolk people accepted them, and they enjoyed much hospitality.

Well, this day was to be one that stayed in my memory for many years. As we entered the pub, everywhere was absolutely packed. One of us tried to get to the counter to buy drinks, but immediately a uniformed arm stretched out and a voice said, 'Gee, you've got to have a drink on us. The war is over. Japan has surrendered!'

Taking this with a pinch of salt, we looked at the lady behind the bar. 'That's right,' she said. 'It's all over. They've surrendered.' We could hardly believe it. All over? My god, we thought, at last! My immediate thought was that now, perhaps, Bill would get home, but it was to be a very long time before he did.

Soon we were all aware of how the atomic bombs had brought a hasty conclusion to a devastating and cruel war. At midnight on August 14th, Clement Attlee announced that the war with Japan was over and V.J. Day began. H.M.S. *Woodcock* was in Tokyo Bay at the surrender of the Japanese fleet. Prisoners were gradually freed from their long imprisonment and brought home on troop ships, liners and warships. We saw pictures of terrible atrocities, and many gaunt figures, who had survived the ordeal, had tales to tell. Most would never forget; some didn't survive the journey home.

The months went by and Bill had no word of his ship's return to England. He wrote to say that he had been to Hiroshima and into some of the camps where men had been held.

As each ship came home, we were given the name of the port it was to arrive at, the time and the berth. I listened anxiously to hear of the *Woodcock*'s arrival. The next thing I heard was that he was due to have an operation in Hong Kong Hospital for appendicitis and dreaded being in hospital when his ship left.

Bill had spoken of getting a nice present for Christopher, but I feared that his appendicitis might have interfered with his plans. On my return visit to Margaret in Devon, she very kindly offered to sell me an electric train set, because she had two. I had a choice, and bought the *Sir Nigel Gresley*. Little did my son know this when we travelled back to Sheringham with all our luggage and the push-chair.

Then we heard that *Woodcock* was to come into Harwich harbour the very next day. Somehow, I managed to get Christopher and myself on to an early train at 6 o'clock in the morning. Bill had written to say that he had refused to go into the hospital in Hong Kong and would have to go into Chatham Hospital as soon as he got home. He would not be getting leave, hence my eagerness to meet his ship. The train quickly filled up with naval ratings when we left Ipswich. At Harwich I had to find his ship; there were hundreds of sailors going in every direction. A sentry came forward and asked what ship I was looking for. When I told him, he pointed towards the river and said, 'That's her, out there.'

He took us to the first vessel alongside the dock. We were soon accompanied by another sailor and walked from one vessel to another, at last reaching the *Woodcock*. A sailor's voice shouted out, 'Lofty Ayers, where is he? His wife is here.'

Bill suddenly appeared, coming down the nearest ladder, and we were shown around his ship, his mess-deck, small caboose, and the guns. We were also introduced to his first lieutenant who was the Earl of Dalkieth. After the introductions, I was offered a glass of sherry which was very acceptable. His Number One then said to us, 'I suppose you want to go home, Ayers?' Of course Bill did, so he then said, 'You've got 24 hours leave. Be in Chatham Hospital after that.'

This was 1946. Bill's time in the Royal Navy was coming to an end. He had joined as a boy of fifteen, going first to H.M.S. *Ganges* and then into the Navy on his eighteenth birthday. His twelve years would end on 10th February 1947, his thirtieth birthday. He didn't want to sign on for further service and longed to be in civvy street.

Early in 1946, Sheringham Urban District Council was preparing to build its first Council houses after the war. It was proposed to build about 26 semi-detached houses on land in Pine Grove. We hoped to be allocated one. As I had put my name down very early on during the war, I felt we had a good chance of getting one quite quickly, but it was not to be.

That winter was a really bad one, with the severest weather since 1940. Bill came home on leave several times, and often we walked by way of the new houses to see the building going on. Several young married couples were allocated houses and I began to think our luck was out as family after family got theirs.

The day for Bill's release from the Royal Navy came, and we had snow everywhere with icy conditions. I had told Christopher he could stay up late that day to see his Daddy come home. On that Monday afternoon the roads were completely clear of snow, but then a very fine sleet arrived with a biting wind. Inside, before a roaring fire, we were completely unaware of the conditions outside. As the time drew near for me to meet his train, I went into the little scullery to be confronted with heaps of snow that had drifted under the back door. I pulled open the door and could see a pile of snow but didn't realize how deep it was.

Carrying long thigh boots, I set forth to meet the train. The roads were covered with drifts of deep snow from one side to the other and it was blowing hard. I managed somehow to get to the station, expecting to see the railway lines as usual. Suddenly a porter appeared and said, 'Whatever are you doing here on a night like this?'

'I've come to meet my husband off the 10 o'clock train,' I said, realizing at the same time that the railway lines were completely covered with snow. It lay several feet deep.

'You wont see him here,' he said. 'He'll have got off at Cromer.' I realized only too well that this was true, and turned homeward. The train, carrying troops and others, was completely snowbound. Bill got home next morning, having got out at Cromer and walked home by the beach. He was very glad to get home and told us he had many weeks leave due to him, foreign service leave plus other leave due to him which would give him until the summer. However, a couple of days later, a postman came to our door and brought a letter from the postmaster asking for help with delivering the mail. 'Only temporary', he said, so Bill didn't like to see them in a muddle and went to oblige them at the Sheringham Office. He little realized then that he was to be there over twenty years. So much for his 'long service' leave, which he sacrificed in order to help out.

Our hopes of getting a Council house in Pine Grove looked bleak. All of them had now been allocated. I had not pursued the Council at all; we just hoped the system was fair. One day I saw one of the councillors who knew me, Mr Henry Bishop, and he said, 'They are going to build some more next year. Perhaps you'll have better luck then. They'll be better anyway.' I felt disappointed as it probably meant waiting another year. We were happy with my mum and dad, but we needed our own place.

Late one evening in March, there was a knock at our door, and a clerk from the council office handed me a letter. We had been allocated a house and we could have the key in April. How very pleased we were. April came and the snow was still on the ground, but despite that we moved in, having got the last house on the estate.

Our life together in civvy street had begun, and the problems and joys of family life lay ahead of us.

They gave their lives

D. Leigh Barratt
Charles Bensley
Mark Bucknall
John R. Bush
Raymond Coward
Stanley A. Craske
John R. Creasey
Royden W. Duffield
Patrick C. Everitt
Harry Farrow
Raymond Fields
Kenneth Finch
Oliver A. Fincham
Frederick Fitch
John A. C. Fitch
David H. Fletcher
Sydney C. Graveling
Robert Greenacre
Charles Grice
Jack Grice
Margaret Grice
Walter W. Harries
Claude Houghton
William R. Howes
John Hyslop
Charles Ireland
Edgar Jenkinson
Frederick C. L. Lennard
Joseph Lenton
Peter S. H. Osborne
George T. Page
Benjamin Reynolds
Frederick Reynolds
Ernest J. Sayer
George Bernard Smith
Geoffrey W. Steward
James W. Tuck
Ernest Webdale
E. P. Wentworth-Dillon